The Symbol of the Dog in the Human Psyche

A Study of the Human-Dog Bond

ELEANORA M. WOLOY

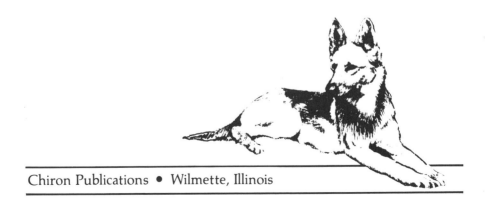

Chiron Publications • Wilmette, Illinois

The Chiron Monograph Series, Volume IV

General Editors: Nathan Schwartz-Salant, Murray Stein
Managing Editor: Harriet Hudnut Halliday

Library of Congress Catalog Card Number: 89-29509

Printed in the United States of America

Book design by Elaine M. Hill

Library of Congress Cataloging-in-Publication Data

Woloy, Eleanora M.
    The symbol of the dog in the human psyche / Eleanora M.
      Woloy.
      p. cm. – (The Chiron monograph series ; v. 4)
    ISBN 0-933029-47-0
    1. Archetype (Psychology) 2. Dogs – Psychological
aspects. 3. Human-animal relationships. I. Title. II. Series
BF175.5.A72W64 1990
155.9 – dc20   89-29509
                                     CIP

Were my Master to grant me but a single glance through these sightless eyes, I would without question choose to see first a child, then a dog.

Helen Keller

Contents

Foreword

There is an ancient contract between humankind and the dog, forged in wordless interchange and mutual respect around uncountable campfires in the distant recesses of early evolution of human forms on earth. In the mind of many of us (mine is one) there is a special place of affection and respect for dogs.

I recall many dogs: a great collie that left the barest trace in my earliest memory; a small black bull called Speedy that was killed by a car in 1939; Puddles and Mack (who were brothers); "Dwag"; Tibothea Hatshep o-long; Tibby II; Katherine-the-Great-Dane; Gritches; Mimi; Toy; Fate; Tar-Jane; Raven; Isis; and others whose names have slipped into the collective sense of dogs who were close companions to my family and me—all of them individuals, all of them more than pets.

The most poignant dog in my memory, however, is Tarzan, a little white spitz that old Dr. Halley (who may have delivered me) got from a litter at one of the oil field camps to replace Speedy, who had been killed just before my mother, my sister, and I left for the Panhandle of West Texas to visit my grandfather's ranch. When I returned home several weeks later for the start of the first grade, Tarzan hid behind the curtains and growled with puppy fierceness.

Tarzan was named for his habit of grabbing the thick rope that hung from the large oak tree in our front yard and growling as he swung and was swung about. He slept in a doll's cradle—borrowed from my sister's room—by the side of my bed. He was very protective and had a fierce temper for anyone he thought intended to harm me. I did not know he was exemplifying all the archetypal meanings of dog.

Tarzan would not eat eggs, but because my basic chore was to feed the chickens and gather the eggs, he went with me each afternoon to the hen house. There he carefully took one egg in his mouth, carried it thirty or forty yards to a flower bed, and there carefully buried it. At our house the April showers would wash up buried eggs in unexpected places; Tarzan would gather them. Was his egg-gathering a rudimentary sense of value? Of money? Of helping me?

He died of dropsy when I was a senior in high school. I cried and buried him more carefully than any of his eggs had been buried in the flower beds.

I accidentally ran over Puddles when I was learning to drive – a real tragedy. Mimi, the poodle, died of old age – living at least a year beyond the time her body was ready to go simply because she hated to leave us. Katherine-the-Dane was the first dog we had "put down," euthanasia being considered only after her neurological wasting disease made her too weak to stand and walk. In retrospect, we waited too long. Gritches was the second to die by decision, when an irreparable disk rupture had paralyzed her hindquarters.

The death of dogs was my first lesson in that awesome final mystery of life. For the first half of my life, people seemed to always outlive their dogs; then, as I neared my own half-century mark, the people began to die also.

There is, in fact, a marked connection between dogs and death. Not the fear of the primordial wolf pack, but a long association that has passed through so many cultures and so numerous generations that it has become archetypal, lodged in the very root structures of the human psyche. In Ancient Egypt, Anubis, the god with the head of a jackal, was the master of mummification – that work on the dead body that was intended to make immortal the soul that had inhabited it. Anubis was the finder-of-ways, the Lord of the Necropolis, the one who could lead the soul to the world of the immortals after death. A further connection between death and dogs can be seen in many medieval churches where one can find the carved tombs of knights in which the feet of the dead master rest on the side or back of the sleeping, faithful dog at his feet.

All this rich depth of association of humankind and dog, so clear in my own personal experience, extends to dogs as "transitional objects" that help in the childhood task of learning to be left alone, as companions of the hunt, as eyes for the blind, as friends for the lonely, and even as dogs employing their sense of smell to find illegal shipments of drugs.

But the most impressive experience of the dog imagery in

my own psyche occurred in a dream the night after my mother's death. In the dream I have a large ring of my mother's keys. I noticed a bit of spider web among them and when I shook the keys, a black widow spider fell to the floor at my feet. A spider, particularly the black widow, is often a symbol of a negative mother complex, which in my case was quite small. Suddenly a dog appeared at my side. It was Tar-Jane, the American Eskimo who had died of heart disease a few months before. She quickly devoured the spider and showed no ill effects. In my dream a tiny, residual negative-mother complex had been removed by that archetypal guide at the time of death, the dog.

Until now there has been no one book that has explored the deeper meaning of the dog with the sensitivity acquired by the practice of Jungian analysis and the interpretation of dreams. Dr. Woloy has masterfully filled this gap. I have followed her effort from its earliest stages and I find it both scholarly and soulful.

I commend this book to those who wish, like me, to follow in scope and detail our enduring contract between humankind and the dog.

James A. Hall, M.D.

Preface

Every early culture had an Earth Goddess with a dog companion. At this time in the development of consciousness when we are reconnecting to lost aspects of the feminine principle, the association of the dog with the Goddess is again an important image to be nurtured and kept alive in the collective consciousness. This is reflected in the dreams of men and women as well as in our current literature, as with the recent book, *Dogs and Their Women,* by Barbara Cohen and Louise Taylor. An image can be a bridge to understanding something that contains mystery because it touches the nonverbal place of understanding, the deep recesses of the psyche where words are often ineffectual.

I view the feminine principle as a psychological process in both men and women which is quite different from the gender we know as female. I define the feminine element as that part of the psyche that is actively receptive and accounts for the ability to be fully present in each moment of life in a way that is just right for that moment. D. W. Winnicott (1971, pp. 80–81) recognized the compelling importance of the female mode of "being" when he declared it an essential part of our humanity for both men and women. It is that part of our humanity that respects relatedness and empathy. It is a way that allows us to embrace ambiguities. It is a way that honors and values our world—both inner and outer.

To understand the new we often have to study the old. Jung stated, "It is only possible to come to a right under-standing and appreciation of a contemporary psychological problem when we reach a point outside our own time to observe it" (1954, p. 166). This is why I have reached back to the ancient myths and early religious rituals. The Eleusinian mysteries, which were a ritual enactment of the Demeter-Persephone myth, were feminine mysteries for both men and women in ancient Greece. These rituals, which were an important part of Greek life from 500 B.C. to about 360 A.D., included a dog.

Patricia Dale-Green in her excellent book *Dog* (1966, p. 122) describes a sculpture representing an Eleusinian cave, which shows the Great Mother Goddess Demeter attended by a dog with an aspirant being brought into the cave by a dog. The Goddess and her dog-companion, as in the myths of Gula, Isis, Hecate, Ishtar, Annuwn, and Hell, represent that aspect of the feminine that is connected to the inner realms of the psyche — otherness — through the instincts. From the awareness of the dog's association to the early goddesses and the dog's part in the early feminine mysteries, I was led to my belief that feminine consciousness is an integral part of the human-dog bond. By understanding this feminine aspect of our connection to dogs in a more symbolic way, we can have a deeper and fuller experience of the dogs that we know and learn more about the archetype, or primordial image common to all humanity, of the human-dog bond. It is through the feminine that we have a deep connection to ourselves; and it is through the feminine that we come to appreciate creatures and things other than ourselves and to which we are ultimately connected.

Acknowledgments

I want to thank the many people who have been helpful to me in developing this book. The work of C. G. Jung has a continuing and profound influence on my life. By example, he has given me permission to pursue my own psychic images. His concept of the *unus mundus*, the unitary world structured by archetypal processes, has given me a framework on which to understand many questions that have concerned me. A great deal of my understanding of the feminine principle has come from the written work and personal discussions with Marion Woodman. The work of Nathan Schwartz-Salant, consisting of the detailed clinical study of narcissistic and borderline personality structures and how these structures relate to mythology and alchemy, has been helpful in understanding the imaginal, relational, and religious aspects of the feminine principle. This understanding has been essential for me to fully comprehend the meaning of the image of the Goddess in association to the dog.

Ronald Kledzik, Paul Kugler, Harriet Machtiger, Meredith Moon, David Sedgwick, Jackie Travers, and the late Michael Vermillion brought to my attention useful material that I had not discovered in my own survey. Dorothy Shaffer led me to the Metropolitan Museum of Art to find the bronze "Diane" I use as the frontispiece. Ruth Goodwin and Lois Khan gave me useful suggestions to make this work more complete. Albert Powell, Jr., and Robyn Browder, who edited the thesis material, gave me suggestions to make the early material more coherent. Jamal Bayati, a scholar on the Muslim religion; Donald Brown, former superintendent of Isle Royal National Park; and Beth and Bob Duman, who raised a wolf, gave me personal interviews that yielded information I have included. I want to thank Loki, a native Hawaiian woman whom I met quite synchronistically in Hawaii and who told me the story of the White Dog of Pele, who is both guide and guardian of the Wiapio Valley. I want especially to thank James Hall and

Murray Stein, who saw value in my thesis material and who encouraged me to rewrite the material into a book. I also want to express my deepest gratitude to my friends at Apple Farm who continue to encourage me. I thank both June Bratcher for allowing me to use material from her family diary and Mitra Dileo for translating the Javad Nurbakhsh work from the original in Persian. My appreciation goes also to my analysands and close friends who allowed me to use their personal material, and to Carole Turner, who patiently did all the typing. And, finally, I could have never completed this book without the understanding of my family, who allowed me time to write and rewrite and who patiently listened to my efforts to make myself clear. To all these people I am most grateful.

Introduction

From 1982 to 1987 my dog, Tinsel, an old female German Shepherd, was with me in my analytic office while I saw analysands. When the image of Tinsel began to appear in the dreams of some of my analysands, I became interested in understanding more about the meaning of the human's relationship to the dog, specifically from the position of depth psychology, that is, the archetypal basis of the dog and its relationship to humankind. Other analysts have kept a dog in their consulting room while seeing analysands: among them were Sigmund Freud, C. F. Baynes, and, more recently, Marie-Louise von Franz and Lois Khan.[1] In the film "The Way of the Dream," in which Fraser Boa interviewed Dr. von Franz concerning symbols and motifs in dreams, her bulldog was present throughout.

A relationship with dogs is something that has roots deep in my own personal life. Both of my parents came from severely deprived backgrounds where keeping a pet was not part of the family experience. Although the animals on our small farm were to be primarily utilitarian—milk goats, barn cats, and chickens—my parents, particularly my mother, really loved and valued the animals, and so the decision was made that I should be allowed to have a dog. The raising, training, and breeding of my German Shepherd, Suchi, during my adolescent years gave me the opportunity for a total unconditional friendship, for learning self-confidence when I showed her in the show ring, and for relating to significant adults outside of my very troubled home environment. I learned about the natural cycles of life through breeding, pregnancy, and caring for puppies; the pain of separation when the puppies had to be sold; and eventually the grief that came when Suchi developed breast cancer and had to be put to sleep. I am not being dramatic when I say that my relationship with Suchi and all that I learned from her was life-saving to me. Had it not been for my involvement with her, I feel I would

1

have been more negatively affected by the depressions of both my mother and father. And, as an adult, my own awareness of the importance of Suchi in my life has made me more sensitive to pets in my analysands' backgrounds, and I often ask about them.

During my twenty-two years practicing as a psychiatrist, I have heard many life stories concerning relationships with dogs, so I know that dogs have had profound influences in the lives of many people. I have found that for some individuals the love of a dog actually carries the life spark or the will to live during certain periods of severe difficulty. In this book I am writing directly from my own experiences of having a dog in my office while working with analysands. I will show how my analysands felt in the presence of that dog and how it presented itself in their dream material, which I analyzed from my understanding of Jungian psychology.

I could have written, but chose not to, an anecdotal report of the many direct experiences between the analysands and the dog. For example, Tinsel seemed to know when to thrust her nose into the lap of a crying analysand and when to get up and simply stand quietly at his or her side. Each time what she did seemed exactly right. She would let some children give their dolls rides on her back even though she was in pain from her arthritic hips, or let them spend their sessions talking with me from the floor, resting their heads on her body. With other children she would rest quietly under the play table. On one occasion she backed away from a man whom I had been seeing for over three years and refused to come into the room with him. That day he had reached a place of psychic fragmentation which became perceptible to me only as he began to talk but which had been instantly perceptible to Tinsel. These, as well as many other experiences, raised questions in my mind about the nature of a dog's perceptions. I have not chosen to address these experiences directly in this book, although I am sure they did influence the dream material. Rather, I am attempting to understand something more of the meaning of the human-dog bond from the dream and sandtray material of my analysands and from the correlation to mythology.

This book has been difficult to write because, particularly in the chapter about my own view of the human-dog relationship,

I am attempting to put into language and word pictures something that really cannot easily be reduced to a verbal description. I am writing about symbols that are the best possible description of something unknown. A symbol always carries in it a little mystery and so cannot be understood solely by rational thinking. Therefore, I have tried to stay within an outline that I hope will by progression help make these views more understandable.

In the two years during which I reviewed psychiatric and psychological literature on the use of the dog in therapy, I found not one reference to Jung nor any allusion to the dog as an archetype. Aaron Katcher, M.D., a psychiatrist at the University of Pennsylvania who has studied the psycho-physiological responses of relaxation in relationship to dogs, uses the concept of archaic inheritance to understand the underlying basis of safety and our trusting relationship to dogs. The concept of archaic inheritance as discussed by Sigmund Freud adumbrated Jung's concept of the archetype but does not begin to contain the richness and fullness of its meaning. I will discuss Katcher's work at length in chapter 2 when I discuss theories of the human-companion-animal bond. I discovered from my readings that it has been only since the late 1960s that there have been scientific observational data about the health and well-being of humans in relationship to their pets. This work has been primarily anecdotal and began when Boris Levinson, a psychologist practicing in New York City, began to notice the salutary effect that his dog, Jingles, would have when the dog would accidentally follow him down from their upstairs apartment and greet the seriously disturbed children with whom he worked.

Serious scientific inquiry with statistical work and with a data base of observational and psychological correlates began in the late 1970s, primarily with the work of Katcher. This topic is of such interest that the American Psychiatric Association included a section entitled "Pets and People—Examining a Complex Relationship" at their 1984 annual meeting in Los Angeles. There have been many unanswered questions raised in the primary observational material, such as, Why will an autistic child respond to a dog but not to another human being? Why does a deaf person talk to an animal but not to another human being? Why will an elderly person, withdrawn for years, respond to a dog and not to the caretakers who are trying to communicate with him or her? In reviewing the current theories about the human-companion-animal bond and by adding to these theories from my own perspective, perhaps I can broaden or add some insight into this complex relationship.

In chapter 1, I deal with the history of the domestication of the dog, with a section that gives attention to the place of the dog in early religious ritual. A review of current thinking about the nature of the human-animal bond appears in chapter 2, since this book would not truly be complete without including the views from the fields of psychiatry, social anthropology, and veterinary medicine. In chapter 3, I explore specific motifs by which the archetype of the dog is expressed in mythology: the helpful animal related to instinct; the dog as a symbol of death and rebirth; the dog as psychopomp, or guide—in all instances the dog is the guide par excellence. Chapter 4 contains dreams of my analysands and a sandtray analysis, all of which are particularly clear representations of the specific motifs. I discuss the archetypal motif and how it fits into the current phase of development of each analysand. And, finally, in chapter 5, I will summarize and present from a Jungian point of view my understanding of the archetypal nature of the human's relationship to dogs and why the image of the goddess with her dog, as shown in the frontispiece, is important for modern men and women.

There is a creation myth reported by Dale-Green (1966, p. 17) which states that after Creation, a gulf opened between Adam and the beasts he had named. Among the beasts stood a dog. When separation was almost complete, it leaped across the gulf, taking its place at the side of man.[2]

I hope that this presentation of how the dog adds to the quality of life for so many people will be of interest not only to those in the helping professions but also to those who simply care about dogs. Perhaps raising consciousness by an awareness of the fuller meaning of dogs in our lives will help us in the overall relatedness between ourselves and the world around us.

Notes

1. Lois Khan has shared with me her experiences from having her Golden Retriever, Buffy, present while she sees analysands. Buffy's incredible emotional attunement to analysands paralleled my experience with Tinsel.

2. Another account came to me from Lois Khan, who had heard this tale from Marie-Louise von Franz:

Long, long ago, animals lived in peace and harmony. Then man came—arrogant, self-willed, and killing for food and fun. Finally all of the animals gathered for council. They decided to combine their efforts and eradicate malicious man while he slept. The dog, hearing the well-laid plans, slipped away into the company of man, giving a warning. The next night when the animals prepared to attack and eliminate man once and for all, they discovered man prepared. They felt the dog had betrayed their cause in saving man and cursed the dog to be dependent on man forever. Thus he became the loyal, faithful companion of people.

Chapter 1

History

> What is man without beasts? If all the beasts
> are gone, man would die from great loneliness
> of spirit, for whatever happens to beasts also
> happens to man. All things are connected.
> Whatever befalls the earth befalls the sons of
> the earth.
>
> *Chief Seattle*

THEORIES OF DOMESTICATION

The dog is thought to be the oldest of domestic animal species, with the earliest fossil remains having been found in Iraq and dating from about 12,000 years ago in the Mesolithic Period of human cultural development, following the end of the last global Ice Age. This was a time of shift from the hunting economies of the Ice Age to the hunting-gathering economies in semi-settled communities following the retreats of the ice caps. It can be inferred from the changes of this transition that conditions allowed for a closer connection between humankind and animals, and that domestication occurred. Domestication refers to a time when humans, rather than just the natural forces, became agents in breeding. As early as 3,500 B.C., carvings on Egyptian tombs and monuments depicted three, perhaps four, well-defined breeds of dogs: the Mastiff, the Hound, the Terrier, and the small Maltese. Exactly how long there had been a relationship between dog and humans is unknown, but fossil discoveries in China indicate a possible association of Peking man and a wolf-like member of the family *Canidae* (which includes dogs, wolves, jackals, and foxes) in the Middle Pleistocene Epoch (from 2.5 million to 10,000 years ago).

A recent discovery of the Yukon Old Crow region placed (by radioactive dating) one cooperative relationship with dogs at 28,000 years (Bustard 1984, p. 21). It is felt that the human capacity to generalize social responses and include wild animals and other species is at the root of the domestication process. Konrad Lorenz has postulated how the first domestication may have begun (1953, pp. 1–13). He surmises that there must have been continual danger in the lives of our early ancestors, both from other hunting tribes and from the larger beasts of prey as well. Jackals[1] probably followed in the tracks of human hordes scavenging the refuse that surrounded the camps, but there was no feeling of friendship uniting the humans with their followers, even though their bark nonetheless warned the humans of some other approaching animal. Perhaps, he states, a group of early humans found themselves without followers, and, tired and sleepless, one man, whose forehead was perhaps a bit higher out of some new intuition, left pieces of their catch on the path to draw the jackals and insure sleep with the feeling of safety. This would have been epic-making as it would be the very beginning of a relationship between humans and dog. But the actual first direct contact with dogs probably was the taking in of an orphaned pup, much as suggested by Jean Auel in her book, *Mammoth Hunters* (1985, pp. 352–53, 379). Wild dogs are by nature very shy, so the caring for and raising of a pup would have been the only way a dog would have been able to have been part of a household.

The Superintendent of Isle Royal National Park, which supports from two to five packs of wolves totally without human intervention, stated that because of the wolves' shyness, he never once saw or heard any of the wolves during the three years he lived on the island. The only way the naturalists have been able to study these packs is from low flying aircraft (Peterson 1977). These observations would support the notion that the first real connection occurred when a pup was taken into a household by a human being.

The theories of domestication of dogs include their use as food, as guards, as hunters, as commensal, and as pets. Although dogs are still eaten as food in parts of the world such as the Far East and the Americas, it is felt that because they are predominantly carnivorous, they make poor propositions as food (when compared with the herbivorous animals); so dogs were probably not domesticated primarily for food.[2] Lorenz's postulated beginning indicates how guarding may have been one of the purposes of domestication, but as time evolved, he also suggests, as Joseph Campbell noted also (1969, p. 138), that man began to recognize the supreme tracking abilities of wild dogs and followed them, taking the best for themselves and leaving the remains for the dogs.

The hunting dog as we know it today is really a very late development in our advanced culture, and the image of the cave man hunting with his horde of dogs is probably nothing more than a romantic idea. Another theory of domestication, commensalism, which is the idea that dogs were encouraged to stay close to man to clean up refuse, is not given much credit because during the Mesolithic Period, when domestication took place, man lived in such small groups that there was not sufficient waste to sustain a permanent population of scavenging animals. The theory that domestication took place on a level other than a strictly utilitarian one is a view supported by many and one that I will amplify in the rest of this paper. The dog easily lends itself to domestication because by nature it is a pack animal and it prefers to deposit its urine and feces in a separate place from its living place and so is easily house-trained.

Domestication spread rapidly throughout societies all over the world during a time of fundamental change in human culture, when, because of the receding ice caps, human groups were able to change from a mobile, competitive hunting group where survival was the only focus possible to groups of people that could be more settled and where a richer form of life was possible. Whereas the useful attributes of hunting, territorial barking, and scavenging may have helped to cement the attachments, these perhaps were not essential to its initial formation, but rather it was the human need to relate to the nonhuman environment and the ability to include others in our social responses that was the key to the bond.

RELIGIOUS RITUAL

Jungian psychology has touched me in a most personal way since it gives me an awareness of a religious instinct through its concepts of the archetype and the collective unconscious. The concept of the archetype will be discussed more fully in chapter 3, but at this point I will simply define the term as common patterns of imaginal representation of instincts, allowing for the reality of the religious instinct, that is, the tendency of the psyche to produce images of central value as a result of the necessity of humans to relate themselves to the world around them.

In the high Alps near St. Gallen and again in Germany near Nurenberg, series of caves containing the ceremonially arranged skulls of cave bears have been discovered dating from the period of the Neanderthal man (living during the earlier Late Pleistocene Epoch)—a coarser, heavier type of human being who was thought to have lived 20,000 to 75,000 years ago (Campbell 1969, pp. 339–341). These caves have also revealed evidence of the ceremonial burials of humans. Some have been orientated to the rising and setting sun, which indicates a kind of solar symbolism related to death. Others show evidence of sacrificed animals, suggesting the idea of a difficult journey.[3] These things suggest that there was already concern about the mystery of death, both for the beast killed and for the human as well. There is evidence to suggest that ritualization itself may be instinctive. B. F. Skinner described an important experiment on behavior in pigeons, whereby the pigeons learned to peck at a lighted window to get food (Kimble 1980, p. 144). The researchers found that the birds developed ritualized behavior in which they repeated every action in sequence since they did not know which action produced the seed: they would circle, bow, flop their wings, and stretch their necks, all in ceremonial sequence.

I am discussing at some length the cave-bear rituals because they were the very first rituals discovered relating to early humans and so were the very beginning of the attempt to structure a relationship to the world and to the animals. The cave-bear rituals preceded development of the dog-sacrifice rituals. Cave bears were not as dangerous to early humans as were the other animals, and in fact they shared their caves with them. The bear's ability to hibernate without food and then to awaken in the spring apparently gave early people an impression of life after death. In addition the upright position of the bear impressed the early people so that a primitive identification occurred binding them together in a special way. Perhaps these influences as well as others yet unknown, contributed to an elaborate ceremony that developed with the preservation of the bear's head.

By the time of Cro-Magnon man, 30,000 to 10,000 B.C., cave markings showed the claw of the bear. This too, it must be remembered, was the period in which the dog was thought to join the human family. Jean Auel, in her book *Clan of the Cave Bear* (1981, pp. 403–12), gives in fictional form a description of the cave-bear ceremony. And it is known that the vestiges of the Paleolithic cult of the bear have been identified and described throughout the Arctic.

The Ainu Bear Festival contains similarities to the later dog sacrifice.[4] The Ainu, which in Japanese means sons of dogs, are a Siberian people who migrated to Japan and now live on a reservation similar to the Indian reservations in the United States. They are a semi-nomadic, Paleo-Siberian fishing and hunting people, but at the same time a Neolithic planting people. For them the bear is still the most important of visiting gods. When the bear cub is caught, it is brought to the village and cared for in the lodge, treated with great affection, even suckled by village women. When it begins to get strong, it is put in a cage until it is two or three years old. Then on a fine September day a festival is held to release the god from the body and return it to the mountains. Everyone dresses in their best clothes. The men wear crowns with images of animals, and fetish sticks are set up on the hearth and worshipped. The man who is to give the feast approaches the bear, asks its pardon, hopes it will not be angry, and tells it an honor is about to be conferred upon it. He addressed it,

Oh you divine one, you were sent into the world for us to hunt. Oh precious divinity, we worship you, hear our prayers. We have fed you and brought you up with great care and trouble all because we love you so. Now you have grown big and we are about to send you to your father and mother. When you get to them please speak well of us and tell them how kind we have been. Please come to us again and we will sacrifice you. (Campbell 1969, pp. 336–37)

The bear is then roped and taken out of the cage and made to walk in a circle around the people. Blunt little bamboo arrows bearing a black and white geometrical design are let fly at him and he is teased until he becomes furious. Then he is tied to a decorated stake. Two strong young men seize him, a third puts a long wooden bit between his jaws, two more men hold his back legs and two his front legs, and one takes the pole for strangling under his throat. The other pole is put above the nape of his neck and a perfect marksman puts an arrow into his heart. The poles are squeezed and the bear is dead. The head is removed with the hide attached and carried into the house and arranged among prayer sticks. A morsel of his own flesh is put beneath his snout along with a hardy helping of fish, mullet dumplings, sake, and a bowl of his own stew. Another speech is then made.

> *Oh, little cub, we give you prayer sticks, dumplings, and fish; please take them to your parents. Go straight to your parents without hanging around on the way. When you arrive say to your parents, "I have been nourished for a long time by an Ainu father and mother and have been kept from all trouble and harm. Since I am now grown up I have returned. Please rejoice." If you say this to them little cub, they will be very happy. (Ibid., p. 337)*

A feast is celebrated. There is dancing and the meat of the bear is eaten. The head is then skinned and set upon a fetish pole. Libations of food continue to be offered to such skulls.

It is supposed that the Neanderthal bear hunter practiced some type of ritual involving the head of the bear, whether it was, as in the case of the Ainu, a symbol of a more powerful being, or master of beasts is not known, but in any event we can detect already the idea of a psychic relation to animals and a sense of death and rebirth.

The dog also became an animal of ritual sacrifice. During the Neolithic Period in the upper Nile about 4,000 B.C., dogs were buried with the dead perhaps as guides to the land of the dead. In China images of dogs wearing harnesses very similar to the harnesses worn by the dogs for the blind (Dale-Green 1966, p. 189) were molded in clay and buried with their masters. In the West African tribes of the Banboro, a man's dogs were killed and buried with him (Hays 1963, p. 307). At some point during the domestication of dogs during the late Paleo-lithic period, they because associated with the Shamans. Joseph Campbell (1969, p. 255) states that dogs were often the animal helpers of a Shaman and were the embodiment of the prophetic gift of the Shaman. It was reported by a Siberian Shaman that the spirits of the cave were invisible to all except a few gifted medicine men and dogs. I feel this is related to the structuring theme of the initiation of a Shaman, that is, death and rebirth. In the Koryok Tribe of Siberia, a post outside the house was smeared with blood and hung with sacrificed dogs so as to invoke the spirits (Hays 1963, p. 413). The Iroquois Indians had a winter festival of a sacrifice of a white dog as a time of renewing visions and for general purification. A white dog was strangled, painted, decorated with wampum, and hung on a pole for five days. On the fifth day the dog was laid on a bench in the long house along with baskets of offerings of tobacco and beans. The people walked around it and told it their wishes and it was sent as a messenger to the creator. The dog was laid on a bark litter, carried around three times outside of the long houses, and ritually burned. This was then followed by a feast, speeches of thanksgiving, and a feather dance (ibid., pp. 450–51). There are clear parallels with the bear ritual: an animal held in esteem, a ritual killing by strangulation, the animal seen as a messenger to the creator, and a celebration. These rituals reveal that the relationship of the dog to death and rebirth has its beginning in very early history.

Notes

1. According to Konrad Lorenz, the northern wolf is not the ancestor of most of our domesticated dogs, as was formerly believed, rather the majority are related to the jackal or various larger wolf-like species of the jackal. Only after early man moved toward the Arctic Circle with already domesticated jackal and dingo-like dogs was there an interbreeding with the northern wolf. Dogs showing both the physical and mental propensities of the wolf are the Eskimo dog the Samoyed, the Russian Lajos, and the Chow Chow (Lorenz 1953, pp. 1–13). Richard Fiennes (1976, pp. 145–61) disagrees with Lorenz

and states that all domestic dogs in all their varieties come from an animal of the ecotype of the Asian wolf (Canis lupus pallipes). Fossil remains found in association with finds of Paleolithic culture have been carbon dated to around 30,000 B.C.

But Professor George Minart states in *The New Dog Encyclopedia* (1970, pp. 282–83) that the origin of the domestic dog seems insoluble. There are close structural agreements between dogs, jackals, wolves, and foxes, yet there are also remarkable differences. The foundation stock of the modern carnivora is from the order Creodonta. The most important form was the family Miacidae of the Eocene period (54 million years ago). Through evolution from the Miacidae came three groups of carnivores. Canoidea was one group from which evolved Canidae-wild dogs, wolves, jackals, foxes; Ursidae-bears; Procyonidae-raccoons, pandas; and Murtelidae-weasels, otters, badgers, skunks minks. By the Pleistocene period (from 2.5 million to 19,000 years ago) wild dogs, wolves, jackals, and foxes existed in their individual types.

2. The practice of dog-eating is felt to have arisen during times of starvation (Fogel 1981, p. 7). This practice still occurs in some places, such as the Philippines and Korea. The Society for the Ethical Treatment of Animals is attempting to call attention to the cruel treatment of these animals. Dog-eating continues among the Oglala, a native American population on the Pine Ridge Indian Reservation of South Dakota, for specific celebration where a dog is ritually killed and eaten and regarded as an exemplary messenger of the people to the Great Spirit. This is described in detail by William and Marla Powers in the *Journal of Natural History* (February 1986, pp. 6–16).

3. In the cave of La Ferrassie, in the Gordogne of southern France, two Neanderthal children were found lying supine and near them a hole filled with the ashes and bones of a wild ox. Our later understanding of this arrangement would interpret this as relating to preparation for a journey (Campbell 1969, p. 342).

4. This festival was described in detail by H. R. Hays in *In the Beginning* (1963, pp. 34–35) and in *The Masks of God: Primitive Mythology,* Joseph Campbell (1969, pp. 334–39).

Chapter 2

The Nature of
Human-Dog Bonding

It really explains why one can love an animal
like Topsy or Jofi with such extraordinary
intensity . . . affection without ambivalence
the simplicity of a life free from the almost-
unbearable conflicts of civilization, the beauty
of an existence complete in itself, and yet,
despite all diversions in the organic development, that feeling of an intimate affinity of an
undisputed solidarity. Often when stroking
Jofi I have caught myself humming a melody
which, unmusical as I am, I can't help recognizing as the Aria from "Don Giovanni"; a
bond of friendship unites us both.

Sigmund Freud

In this chapter I will discuss some of the current thinking
about the human-dog bond and how these views connect
with the archetype.

ATTACHMENT AND USE AS A TRANSITIONAL OBJECT

Edward Rynearson (1978, pp. 150–55), a psychiatrist in Seattle, presented a paper at the 1984 American Psychiatric Association meeting suggesting that the nature of the human-dog
bond was in the nature of a basic reciprocal attachment. He
found a neurophysiological matrix common to dogs and
humans because both are mammals that by nature live in
packs, with attachment being of crucial importance. The drive
and need for attachment is a biological instinct separate from
the instincts of sexuality, aggression, dominance, and territo-
riality. It is an instinct based on nurturance, care-giving, and
emotional and physical closeness.

John Bowlby (1969) pioneered work showing that bonding is instinctual rather than being a secondary drive, as suggested by Freud in the early part of his work.[1] When the natural needs for attachment are not met because of unavailability in the environment, there may be regressed attachment needs from this period. These needs show themselves either by anxious attachment behavior, such as over-dependency and clinging, anxious attachment because of fears of abandonment, or by the reaction formation of excessive care-giving. This may account for the somewhat obsessive care given to some pets. In this sense it would be a projective identification — a person's projecting a part of the self onto the pet, then the caring for the pet comes to represent an attempt to care for the self. In the early attachment between mother and child, there has to come the inevitable separation to allow for growth and development. In relationship to pets, there is a similar need to separate and grow. Since the life span of a pet is so much shorter than the human life span, the experience of separation from the pet can allow for a healing of earlier experiences of separation. Separation and growth is an ongoing aspect of our humanity. However, when there is a fixation at some point early in life because of severe trauma and the separation cannot be negotiated, then we may have situations which result in inappropriate compulsive care-giving to pets as well as inconsolable grieving at the time of the pet's loss.

The pet too can be in a sense a transitional object — that is, an intermediary for expressing wants, fantasies and aggressive ideas. D. W. Winnicott in *Playing and Reality* (1977, pp. 11–12, 14) states that the transitional object and the transitional phenomenon start all human beings off with what will always be important to them, i.e., a neutral area of experience that will not be challenged. The transitional object is the original "not me" possession.

Boris Levinson (1969, pp. 41–42), a New York psychologist, found that the presence of a pet during sessions facilitated contact with patients, particularly those who were uncommunicative. He presented a case of pet therapy in 1961 to the annual convention of the American Psychological Association. His presentation was met with much skepticism at that time, but by 1984, as mentioned above, a whole section of the annual meeting of the American Psychiatric Association was devoted to the complex relationships between humans and their pets. There are now several multidisciplinary societies devoted to the use and understanding of animals as used in the fields of mental health.[2] Levinson feels that the dog is the most preferred pet because a dog is most like us. He states that a dog can act as a transitional object. A dog lives in a natural way unless it has been abused by humans. Therefore, interaction with a dog allows children a way of responding to and accepting certain instincts, such as sexual feelings, sibling rivalry, dealing with aggression, and the naturalness of bowel habits. As children develop tolerance of the dog's difficulties, they develop tolerances of their own inabilities. A dog can be a mirror in which children may see themselves loved, not for what they should be or should have been, but for what they are. Acceptance is total. The dog also allows a child to be master. When confronted with reality too painful to face, a dog may indirectly gratify instinctual needs that cannot otherwise be met. But, the close identification with humans has also often made the dog a scapegoat: humans derive ego gratification by passing on to the dog the indignities they must receive in silence from others. In scolding the dog, a potentially dangerous grievance can be dissipated, but this displacement can also be the source of animal abuse by the severely maladjusted (Bossare 1944, pp. 28–48). On the other extreme, the sentimentality caused by not recognizing the difference between humans and the dogs can lead to absurd treatment of the animals, such as reflected in a statement made by one patient, "I do love chocolate cherries so much that my dog must love them too."

The early work reported about the influence of dogs on patients was primarily antidotal and about socializing influences. Aaron Katcher of the University of Pennsylvania began to study the effects of dogs on humans in a more scientific way. He found that keeping a pet is both statistically normal and culturally normative, and that over one-half of the families in the United States keep pets and feel they are important in family life. In the random viewing of over 25,000 photos, he has found that 5 percent contained a person and an animal occupying the center of the photo, that the head of the person was often placed next to the head of the animal, and that the person wore a very relaxed facial expression (Katcher 1984). In a study with children, Katcher found that the pulse and blood pressure was lowered significantly in a child who was brought into a room for an interview in which a dog was also present (ibid.). He found a similar decrease in the heart rate and blood pressure of people petting dogs (in Fogel 1981, p. 58). He discovered as well that men pet dogs as frequently as women, leading him to conclude that perhaps in western culture this is an acceptable way for men to openly express their affection (ibid., pp. 58–62). It is already recognized that people who are single, widowed, or divorced have a higher death rate than people who are married, but Katcher also showed that in white subjects hospitalized for coronary artery disease, the presence of a pet was the strongest social predictor of survival for one year after hospitalization (ibid., p. 48). And, finally, Katcher measured the blood pressure of individuals talking to their pets and found again a decrease in blood pressure. His findings showed 80 percent of people owning animals talk to their pets (ibid., pp. 52–56).

Katcher concluded from these studies that safety and intimacy are the organizing concepts behind our bond to dogs, reminiscent of a time when our ancestors could feel safe when they saw a resting animal—a signal that there was no danger present. This concept correlates psychologically with Freud's idea of "archaic inheritance," which he discussed in *Moses and Monotheism* (1939, pp. 123–33) and which came close to Jung's idea of the archetype (1971, pars. 743–54), which I will discuss in detail in the next chapter. Freud states that thought-processes and whatever may be analogous to them in the id are in themselves unconscious and obtain access to consciousness by becoming linked to mnemonic or memory residues of visual and auditory perceptions along the path of the function of speech. These mnemonic residues are unconscious and operate from the id. He stated that a fresh complication of understanding our behavior arises when we become aware of the probability that what may be operative in an individual's cycle of life may include not only experiences but also things innately present at birth—elements with a phylogenetic origin, that is, an archaic heritage. As evidence of this Freud uses the universality of symbolism and language. Although there has been no proven evidence in biological science, he states, we cannot imagine an inherited tradition based on communication without the survival of memory traces from previous generations. He felt evidence was strong enough to at least postulate—if not scientifically prove—such a fact.

By assuming archaic heritage, Freud states we are also diminishing the gulf which periods of human arrogance have torn too wide apart between mankind and the animals. The theory of instinct in animals is that they bring the ancestral experience of their species with them into their present existence. The archaic heritage of humans corresponds to the instincts of animals, even though different in compass and content. Freud suggested that a memory enters the archaic heritage first if it is repeated often enough and if it is important enough, or both, and it is retrieved from the unconscious by an awakening of a forgotten memory. Freud discussed this idea specifically around his ideas of the primal father who was both loved and feared by his sons because he kept the women for himself and was finally killed by his sons (1913, p. 141). He felt this caused anxiety in children around the Oedipal and castration issues beyond the experience of their own lives. It was because of the archaic heritage that a child's new experiences are intensified, according to Freud, because they are repetitions of some primieval phylogenetic experience.

THE DOG AS A SYMBOL OF THE FIRST BOND

Another view of the human-dog bond is described by Constance Perin, a cultural anthropologist (in Fogel 1981, pp. 68–88). She began by studying the attitude toward dogs of a group of people in a middle-class American neighborhood. She found two groups of dog owners. The negligent dog owners, even though claiming to be devoted to their dogs, often did not have licenses for them, or abandoned them on country roads when they no longer could care for them, or let them run off where they could get lost or killed, or let them mate indiscriminately. Responsible dog owners, on the other hand, besides not abandoning their dogs or neutering dogs not used specifically for breeding purposes, were able to do all the things that negligent dog owners found impossible. The responsible dog owners trained their dogs not to bark when left alone, to walk on a leash, to sit and stay, thus protecting children and older people from being jumped upon. They did not let their dogs roam where they could cause disturbances or turn over trash or where the dog was subject to danger. Perin related the difference in these two groups of dog owners to early parental relationships and the negotiation of the early process of separation and individuation.

In our Western world one theory of the process of separation from mothers follows the pattern defined by Margaret Mahler (1975, pp. 52–120), which includes a period of symbiosis with visceral feelings of intimacy and comfort; then a period of differentiation with feelings of self-confidence and autonomy and a long period of practicing and rapprochement; and, finally, the awareness that the child most cope with the world on his or her own, unable to command relief simply by feeling the need or giving voice to it. This disappointment at having to give up something once held, the tug between remaining in close touch and moving off in the world, is the mainspring of the eternal struggle against both fusion and separation. The life cycle may be seen as the process of distancing from the real mother but introjecting the symbolic mother, who is part of oneself, in a state of well-being.

Perin suggests that we reach across species and idealize dogs because in no human relationship can we re-create this symbolic vessel of excess love. Dogs give complete and total love—speechless, yet communicating perfectly; mute, but ever attending. The relationship then becomes the memory of the hope for a magical once-in-a-lifetime bond. Attempting to re-create this in relationships with other people can create static and problems in intimacy. The fact that humans reach across species is fundamental to Perin's ideas, as reaching symbolizes the reality of the original separation and allows for coming to terms with the inevitableness of the loss inherent in a first relationship without losing faith in other subsequent ones. She feels that perhaps the irresponsibility of the negligent dog owners is caused by the archaic resurrection of the early parent relationship and triggers anger resulting in the ambivalence in the attitude toward their dogs. Responsible dog owners may struggle no less with the fundamental issues of life-closeness, separation, and disappointment but they have chosen another vehicle with which to work this out. Perhaps we can better understand the statement of James Agee and Evans Walker, "Man has been inspired to call dogs, in competition only with his mother, his best friend" (1966, p. 86).

THE DOG AS A CONNECTION TO NATURE

Harold Searls (1960, p. 120), as well as Rynearson (1978), Bowlby (1969), and Levinson (1969), also views dogs as a transitional object, but at a much deeper level than implied by Levinson. He, as well as Katcher (1984) and Lorenz (1953), sees dogs in a mediating role between humans and nature. Such psychoanalytic literature as there has been has usually stressed the importance of pets, particularly of the dog, as serving as substitutes for other human beings through transference and projection rather than stressing a relatedness to the dog innately as a separate biological being. The following is an example of such literature:

> *The domesticated animal, in particular the dog, is for civilized man what the totem animal was for the primitive. The dog represents a protector, a talisman against the fear of death which is first experienced as separation anxiety. Since separation anxiety gives rise to an increase in the cannibalistic drives, the dog is also in that sense a protector. By displacement, projection, and identification, a dog may serve as a factor in the maintenance of psychological equilibrium. (Heiman 1956, p. 223)*

Searls (1960, p. 160), in contrast, points out that a dog as a dog is of real significance to human beings and that they are capable of entering into human emotional relationships bilaterally. The dog is the object that is a repository of symbolic meaning; that is, we can relate to it transferentially. But it is also a living being that eats, bites, destroys, urinates, lavishes affection, has a sexual life, and is subject to life and death so we can relate to it as itself. It is through a dog that we have an opportunity to relate to the non-human environment, which paradoxically gives us a sense of the unity of all things. In our process of becoming individual we struggle to differentiate ourselves fully from others around us as well as from our environment, and in the proportion that we differentiate—that is, develop consciousness—there can be an increased awareness of relatedness to others and the world around us. The dog may serve as this link. This sense of unity is what Jung (1955, pars. 660-61, 663-64) referred to as the *unus mundus*, the unitary reality, the one world.

Notes

1. Sigmund Freud's secondary-drive theory suggests that the infant's attachment to the mother is secondary to the satisfaction of physiological needs (1905, p. 180). Although Freud did not move away from the secondary-drive theory, there were suggestions in his writing that component instincts built into human nature during the course of evolution underlie the first love experience.

2. The Delta Society is a nonprofit, multidisciplinary group of professionals of interrelated fields, formed specifically for the purpose of research and understanding the relationship among people, animals, and the environment. The Delta Society published its first journal in the fall of 1984.

Chapter 3

The Dog in Mythology

> Of all the animals, the dog is the most com-
> pletely adapted to man, is the most responsive
> to his moods, copies him, and understands
> what is expected of him. He is the essence of
> relationship.
>
> *Marie-Louise von Franz*

Chapter 1 presented the history of the domestication of the dog and the way in which the dog became part of the ritual of religious ceremony in the early humans' need to relate themselves to life and death and the world around them. This need to relate forms the religious instinct of today, coming from the deepest layers of being and resulting in the creation of religious images, concretized in ceremonies throughout the epics of time. These primordial images, called "archetypal images" by Jung, come from the deep layers of the human unconscious. Archetypes are the building blocks of the imaginal psyche, and there are as many archetypal images as there are typical human experiences. The archetype should be regarded as an energy field underlying the psychic process of transforming instincts into images that can be symbols. Archetypes are the collective structural dominants of the unconscious which come into existence with life itself. They are the living forces that regulate, shape, and transform sheer instinct by changing it into mental forms or images and thus are responsible for our ideas and creative productions. Jung's specific contribution to the idea of the archetype was that these organizing principles have a numinous effect, that is, a richness and fullness of meaning that is felt in the images. "The *numinosum* as a dynamic agency is not caused by an act of will. On the contrary it seizes and controls one and is experienced as a quality belonging to a specific object, or as an influence of an invisible presence" (Jung 1958, par. 6). The captivation of the psyche by the numinous provides a shift, or change, in psychic energy so that new meaning can come into consciousness.

Jung was well versed in philosophy, world literature, and primitive cultures and developed his ideas about archetypes as he observed the common motifs or patterns in world religions, primitive ceremonies, myth, and fairy tales as well as in the dreams and psychotic experiences of his patients. Jung often referred to the archetype as being "like the axial system of a crystal" (1959, par. 155). The basic form is part of our instinctive inheritance in the deepest layers of the psyche, the collective unconscious, but the richness and the variety of the images around each basic form or motif attest to the uniqueness and creativity in the psyche of each individual. It is with this in mind that I world like to discuss some of the specific motifs or archetypal forms in which the dog has been represented in mythology.

THE HELPFUL ANIMAL: INSTINCTS

Jung views instincts as the vital foundations that govern all life. Theriomorphic symbols, that is, symbols represented in animal form, always refer to unconscious manifestations of libido or life energy (Jung 1956, par. 261). Regression caused by repressing the instincts leads back to a phase of childhood where the decisive factor appears to be, and sometimes actually is, the parents. The lack of discrimination in a child makes it possible for the animals, which represent the instincts, to appear at the same time as the attributes of their parents so that the motif of the helpful animal may be connected to the parental imago or mental representation of the parent (ibid., par. 265 n.11). If the regression goes still further back beyond the phase of childhood to the preconscious prenatal phase, then archetypal images appear no longer connected with the individual's memories but belong to the stack of inherited possibilities of representation that are born anew in every individual. Jung called this the collective unconscious. The guise in which these figures appear depends on the attitude of the conscious mind: if it is negative toward the unconscious, the animal will be frightening; if positive, it will appear as the "helpful animal" of fairy tale and legend (ibid., par. 264). As I discuss these specific motifs, there will be an interweaving of instincts in the form of the helpful animal and its connection to death, and then to new life as it becomes the psychopomp, or guide.

THE HELPFUL ANIMAL:
COMPANION TO THE HEALING GOD AND GODDESS

According to Greek mythology, the dog was a companion to Asclepius, the legendary god of medicine. Apollo was angry that Coronis, his wife, had been unfaithful and ordered her burned but he removed his son, Asclepius, at the time of her death and gave him to Chiron, the centaur, half man and half horse, to raise. Chiron had the knowledge of music and surgery, and thus Asclepius became the god of healing. In addition, this myth proclaims in it the essence of medicine—out of death comes birth—which I touched on in chapter 2 in regard to religious rituals and which I will explore further in discussing the dog as psychopomp. But I feel it is easy to understand at this point why in ancient cultures healing was often part of a religious ritual and the medicine man and spiritual leader of a group were often the same.

In the narrative by Ovid, around 295 B.C., a plague broke out in Rome believed to be due to the wrath of Apollo (Kerenyi 1959, pp. 14–18). In accordance with an ancient principle of homeopathy expressed in the famous saying of the oracle of Apollo, "The wounder heals," a temple was built to Apollo. His son, Asclepius, was invited to come to Rome from Epidaurus, the home of the healing temple of Asclepius. (See fig. 1.) Asclepius turned himself into a serpent who made his way from the harbor of Epidaurus and boarded a Roman ship of his own accord, choosing the Tiber Island as his destination. The god of the Tiber Island was Faunus, the wolf, who swam out to meet the snake as soon as he arrived.[1] It is important to note that the Tiber Island was also a place of religious significance because on it grew wheat which was sacred to Ceres, goddess of the harvest. Although this myth is centering around events taking place around 295 B.C., it is clearly connecting the snake, the dog, the goddess, and healing, which are images referring to a much earlier time around 2,500 B.C. when the Sumarian goddess Gula was known as the great physician and was depicted as seated on a throne with a dog beside her as the restorer of the dead to life (Dale-Green 1966, p. 95). As an earlier dog deity she appears with a dog's head and was originally called Bau from the dog's bark (Johnson 1988, pp. 115, 184). Gula-Bau, one of the principal deities of the Akkadian and Babylonian peoples, was worshiped particularly as goddess of the grain and lived in a garden at the center of the world with a tree around which a serpent was coiled. A Chaldean cylinder seal from around 2,500 B.C. shows a snake rearing itself from behind the seated goddess (Johnson 1988, p. 184). The goddess was gradually replaced by a god and the dog lost its position to the snake, which remains today on the caduceus, our symbol of medicine.

Elements of these earlier times continue in our current myths. There is a saga reported by Freda Kretschmer that Asclepius himself was suckled by a dog (Hannah 1953–54, p. 3). The dog as a healing animal companion to Asclepius is attested to on two inscriptions in the temple of Asclepius in Epidaurus, which can still be read today. The first concerns a blind child and says, "This child was looked after by one of the temple dogs and left cured." The second reads, "One of the sacred dogs took care with its tongue of a child who had a tumor on its head."

THE HELPFUL ANIMAL: COMPANION TO ISIS

In Egyptian mythology, Isis and Osiris provide another example of the dog as the helpful animal. The Egyptian religion of Isis and Osiris dates back to at least 3,000 B.C. (Harding 1976, p. 168). The Egyptian year consisted originally of only 360 days, but Thoth added five days, making the solar year 365 days. He added these days in July, when Sirius, the dog star, was in ascendance. The dog star was considered to be the attendant of Isis and was her guardian. It also represented Osiris, her consort. During these five days, Nut, the Mother of the Gods who had united secretly with Seb, the master of time, was able to bring forth her children. On the first day she brought forth Osiris; on the second, the elder Horus from the union of Isis and Osiris in the womb; on the third, Set, who

Figure 1 **Silver Coin from Epidaurus, 350 B.C., Bearing Effigy of Asclepius**

leaped forth from her side; on the fourth, Isis; and on the fifth, her sister Nephythys.[2]

Set was always unruly and unmanageable and was forever an enemy of Osiris. Nephythys had only clandestine meetings with Osiris and it was from this union that Anubis, the jackal-headed god, was born.[3] Nephythys was then married to her brother Set, and Osiris became the husband of Isis. When Osiris became king, he taught the Egyptians agriculture, wine-making, laws, and how to honor the gods. But Set laid out a plot to destroy Osiris. He made a casket exactly the right size for Osiris and then invited all the gods to a feast, during which he displayed the casket, which was roundly admired. He promised to give it to whomever it should fit, so they all lay down in it in turn. When Osiris lay down in it, Set's men ambushed him, fastened down the lid, and threw the coffin into the Nile. When Isis heard what had happened, she put on her mourning dress and wandered everywhere, weeping and searching for the casket. She got news from the babbling of children who had seen it float by. Then her dog, Anubis, the child of Nephythys and Osiris, led her to the place where the coffin had floated ashore and come to rest by a heather bush. Its growth had been so stimulated by the presence of the coffin that the tree had grown all around the coffin and enclosed it in its trunk. The king of this land had found the tree and made it into a roof tree for his palace. When Isis reached the palace, she removed the casket form the tree trunk and left with it to find her son Horus, whom she hoped could help her bring Osiris back to life. While she was searching for Horus, Set opened the casket and tore the body of Osiris into fourteen pieces and scattered them about. It was Anubis again and Isis' sister Nephythys who helped her find the pieces of the dismembered body; they put it back together again with their tears. This is yet another ancient myth that links together the goddess and dog.

THE HELPFUL ANIMAL: COMPANION TO THE FOOL

Further example of the dog as the helpful animal is the dog used on the tarot card (see figs. 2, 3, 4, and 6). Tarot is French for a specific deck of cards, and today the tarot deck consists of 78 cards in two parts. The first 56 are the minor trumps and the other 22 cards are the major trumps. No one really knows the original purpose of the cards, but in the eighteenth century, Count de Gebelin viewed the tarot as the primeval hieroglyphics of the Book of Thoth. Etteilla of the same century viewed the cards for the purpose of interpreting dreams and visions (Newman 1983, p. vi). In the nineteenth century they were considered by Gerard Encausse to be the key to all occult sciences (ibid., p. vi). A. E. Waite, the most famous of the twentieth-century commentators, sees the tarot as a series of images that can unlock vast regions of the soul and the unknown (ibid., p. vi). It seems clear that the tarot represents a series of archetypal images inspired from the collective unconscious. The most powerful of all the tarot trumps is the Fool. It is the only card from the tarot that remains in the current deck of playing cards (as the joker). The Fool has no fixed number; in tarot usage he is a wanderer connecting two worlds—the everyday contemporary world where most of us live, and the world of the nonverbal imagination, the place of the archetypes. The Fool repre-

LE MAT
THE FOOL

Figure 2 **Marseilles Tarot Deck**

sents the court jester of the King, which was a privileged position. The Shakespearean Fool could act as an alter ego to the king, as found in King Lear (Kirch 1966, p. 214). The Fool and the dog are closely linked, and portraits of court jesters usually picture them with dogs. "One can imagine that the relationship between these two court animals must have been an intimate one for they were in a sense siblings" (Nichols 1980, p. 24). In many tarot decks the Fool is shown with a small dog nipping at him (compare the Marseilles tarot card [fig. 2] with the Waite version [fig. 3], early twentieth century). The dog appears to be trying to communicate something. The Fool seems to be in such close contact with his instincts that his animal side literally guides his steps, thereby revealing how closely linked the helpful animal is with the instinctual. In con-

Figure 3 **Waite Tarot Deck**

trast with the Waite version, which pictures a young man about to go out on a journey, in the Old French tarot (see fig. 4), the Fool is blindfolded, which indicates a voluntary willingness both to forgo a dependence on the outer eye and to move toward a contemplative life with an inner eye, and to trust the companionship and guidance of his dog. In this sense this figure is the Wise Old Man. Von Franz equates the Fool with "a part of the personality or even of humanity which remains behind and therefore still has the original wholeness of nature" (Hillman and von Franz 1971, pp. 6, 7). In this way the dog seems a natural companion to the Fool.

Another way to look at the dog jumping up from behind, as suggested by Newman (1983, pp. 112–13), would be to see the dog not as a helpful instinct but rather as an instinctual attack from the unconscious, exposing one's human nature. Newman also sees the dog as a motivating instinct neither helpful nor attacking but as a way of being driven onward. Von

Figure 4 **Old French Tarot Deck**

Franz writes of this instinct within the archetypal process of individuation when she writes, "there seems to be a tendency in man to reach a further level of reflection and consciousness, and this comes from instinct and not always from outer disturbing factors alone" (1970, pp. xiii-4).[4] In this view individuation is seen in a less-romanticized way as something that must be suffered, and the Fool is viewed as the wanderer, the stranger, the lonely man suffering his own fate, being driven by his instincts.

The fact that the Fool has no number in the playing cards but is zero, the circle, is also significant in reference to the dog and how it connects to the feminine principle. The power of the zero is inherent in its circular form. To draw a circle there must always be a central point. The center must always come first, and the circle is a natural form of nature. A circle with a dot in the center is a universal sign for the sun, and this hieroglyph is also the sign of the World Egg. The circle is natural to nature and is a symbol of the feminine principle, while a perfect square is found nowhere in nature but is manmade and is a sign of the masculine principle. The circle contains the nothing from out of which all things come, the Great Round as the Great Mother with woman = body = vessel = world (Neumann 1945, pp. 43–45). It is easy to understand why from the very earliest times of recorded mythology the goddess was accompanied by a dog. The details of the association of the goddess to dog will be given under the discussion of the archetype of dog as manifested in life and death.

I want to add here in this discussion of the connection of the dog to the fool or clown figure the fact that among the Oglala Sioux Indians there remains to this day at the Pine Ridge reservation in South Dakota the ceremonial sacrifice and eating of dogs. It is a continuation of an ancient sacred ritual, much as described in chapter 1. The dog sacrificed is regarded as an exemplary messenger of the people, and the dog's spirit carries the people's prayers for health and long life for all their relations. One of the special occasions at which a dog is sacrificed and eaten by this tribe is at the ritual for the Fraternal Society of the Heyoka, the clown or the fool of the tribe (Powers 1986, pp. 6–16).

THE HELPFUL ANIMAL: MODERN TIMES

There is now a broad range of ways that dogs are used in therapy. In many states there are active programs supported by breed clubs and animal shelters, where dogs are taken into homes for the aged on a regular basis. Researchers such as Lynch (1977) and Katcher (in Fogel, 1981) have shown a positive correlation between longevity after heart attacks and reductions in high blood pressure, based on interactions with pets. It is felt that, because dogs are the most social of all animals, bringing them into nursing homes can improve the quality of life by creating a feeling of being needed for those who have given up the will to live (Schwartz 1985, pp. 37–42).

With the current trend toward providing for handicapped individuals in their homes rather than in institutions, a number of nonprofit organizations have arisen. Canine Companions for Independence, based in Santa Rosa, California (founded in 1975); Handi-Dogs in Tucson, Arizona (founded 1974); and Aid Dogs for the Handicapped Foundation in Oreland, Pennsylvania (founded 1969) — all assist the handicapped to train their own dogs to help with the daily tasks of picking up dropped items, opening elevators doors, and turning light switches on and off.

The seeing-eye dog has long represented the epitome of service. The concept of guide dog for the blind was introduced to America in 1919 by Morris Frank, who was wounded in Europe and returned with his European-trained guide dog. He was so impressed with this dog that he founded the first "Seeing-Eye School" in his hometown of Nashville, Tennessee. Later the school was moved to Morristown, New Jersey, where it is today and has become a leader in the service use of dogs, showing the close relationship that can exist between humans and dogs.

The Hearing Dog Program is another organization that provides assistance to people. Dogs are taken from animal shelters, trained and given free of charge to hearing-impaired people. Now 37 of our 50 states recognize hearing dogs and give them the same rights as seeing-eye dogs.

Individual classroom teachers such as Sue Myles of Newport Beach, California, and Cheryl Rahaman of New Platz, New York, are using dogs to help socialize autistic children. These efforts are based on the premise that "the child who participates in his dog's socialization is attuned to the necessity of his own socialization" (Schwartz 1984, p. 73).

In 1982 Leo K. Bustard, Dean of the College of Veterinary Medicine at Washington State University, along with Kathy Quinn, who is active in pet therapy, conceived of an idea of using prison inmates to help train dogs for the handicapped. This program has proved to be an overwhelming success both in giving a sense of purpose to inmates as well as in training otherwise-discarded dogs. Funds are being obtained to build a kennel and make this a full-time part of the prison program (ibid., p. 89).

Rescue dogs are used in Europe and Australia, where they are known as "avalanche dogs." In the United States the American Rescue Dog Association is a national organization consisting of units throughout the country. Their primary use in the United States is to find lost people, children who wander away from home, old people who are disoriented, hunters who are lost, or murder victims. It seems that humans shed over 50 million cells daily from which are emitted volatile gasses as the by-product of the bacteria working on these cells. These gases are carried in a cone around us because of the updraft from the heat of our bodies. This cone of particles is then carried by wind currents so that we leave a trail of specific scent wherever we go, and a dog, because of the shape of its nose and concentration of receptor sites, is able to follow this scent. The bloodhound is the most familiar and for many conjures up the image of a poor prisoner being chased by a vicious dog. In fact the bloodhound is extremely gentle and is more apt to lick the found victim to death than to bite him (Conniff 1986, p. 65). The American Rescue Dog Association uses primarily German Shepherds and has handlers who are highly trained in wilderness navigation to do this work. After the 1988 earthquake in the Soviet province of Armenia, two rescue dogs from an Alaskan team were used in finding victims buried by the disaster.

Dogs have been used for herding and guarding livestock for thousands of years in most of Europe, the British Isles, Russia, Australia, and Asia. Currently studies are being undertaken at the Wildlife Research Center in Denver to come to a better understanding of the effective use of dogs as guards to keep predators from livestock in our western plains states. For example, the Komandorak, originally bred in Hungary as guard dogs for sheep because they look so much like a sheep, has recently been introduced to sheep farms in these states.

The dogs that are best known for their service are the police K-9 dogs. The value of these dogs is something that cannot even be estimated. Their versatility in patrol, attack, disaster search, protection, building search, crowd control, narcotics, explosives, and weapon detection indicates the capabilities the dog has and its willingness to use them to serve a human to whom it is bonded.

Two current uses of a dog's olfactory sensitivity are for

bovine estrus detection and for detecting narcotics. The U.S. Department of Agriculture has conducted research to show that the dogs trained to smell the cows and then sit behind a cow in estrus, are 94 percent correct in detecting the day of estrus. Used in this way, the dog could help the dairy industry cut out needless waste of labor and money. The U.S. Customs Service uses dogs to detect narcotics, dangerous drugs, and hidden weapons and explosives.

In 1981 New York State authorized the use of unleashed tracking dogs to locate wounded game. Deer Search, Inc., was founded to track wounded deer that had been shot and wounded by hunters but not killed. The founder of Deer Search, John Jeanneney of Long Island, New York, had searched a whole day to find a deer he had wounded while hunting. This was the impetus for him to work toward founding the association.

A final way in which dogs can be of help to humans is in their ability to detect a coming earthquake, since they have been known to exhibit unusual behavior just before an earthquake because of ion changes in the air (Schwartz 1980, pp. 106–8).

THE DOG AS A SYMBOL OF LIFE AND DEATH

The Dog and Goddesses

I have already discussed the dog as companion to Gula and Isis. In addition, Erich Neumann states in *The Origins and History of Consciousness* that "the Great Mother rules the animal world of instincts which ministers to her and to her fertility. The male votaries of the Great Goddess were called Kelobim, meaning dogs" (1954, p. 61). The Great Mother gives birth to all, and it is she to whom all return in death. Dogs became closely associated with funerary customs and death probably because they are carrion eaters. There were packs of wild dogs that roamed the streets in early times eating whatever they could find, and there were rabid and plague-carrying dogs that posed a real threat. This association with death caused the dog and the dark side of the Great Mother also to be closely linked. In every tradition the dark or death side of the Goddess is

Figure 5 **Hercules and Cerberus, ca. 510 B.C.**

linked to the dog. In Greek mythology, the death-goddess was Hecate, and her companions were dogs. She was often depicted as three headed and her place of worship was the crossroads, the place of liminality or transition. A crossroads symbolizes the union of opposites, and it was there that the offerings were made, often in the form of dog sacrifices. Hecate, the goddess of the moon, earth, and lower world and triple-bodied goddess of dogs, is identical with Cerberus, the triple-headed guardian of the gates of Hades, although in figure 5 he is seen with only two heads showing (Jung 1956, par. 355).

Thus the dog became a threshold animal, its place being at the gateway to the underworld, at the boundary between life and death. In Norse mythology, Garm (with a bloody chest) was chained to the entrance of the infernal regions until the end of the world. In Greek mythology, Cerberus was the controller. In Hindu mythology, the sun and moon dogs of Indra guarded the gates of the kingdom by night and day. In Persian mythology, there were two four-eyed dogs who guarded the Chinvot Bridge (the Bridge of Decision) between the two worlds. In Native American mythology, the tribes of the Iroquois, the Huron, the Massachusetts Ojibwa, the Seminole, and the central Eskimo have included stories of such guardian dogs. In this position at the crossroads, the dog transmutes instinct into spirit, thus bringing rebirth. Jung states that "because of its rich symbolic context the dog is an apt synonym for the transforming substance" (1963, par. 174, n. 280). This was the meaning of the dog as interpreted in alchemical texts.

This concept of the dog being a transforming substance, as well as the dog's connections to the dark side of the goddess, brings together the dog's association to the moon. Perhaps because of the dog's habit of howling at the moon, they emerged early as the principal animal of the moon. Since plants grow at night, ancient peoples believed the moon activated their growth. Through its connection with the moon, the dog's boundless energy was thought to initiate the growth of sleeping vegetation in springtime, animating and vivifying it.

> On the strength of its moon and caterpillar link pictured on several Cucuteni vases of the fourth millennium B.C., the dog is included among the animals of renewal and transformation. (Johnson 1988, p. 115)

In fact, on the tarot trump card 18, which is the card of the moon, the conventional picture is of two dogs howling at the full moon in front of a gate, a symbol of a place of passage, again showing the association of the dog to transition (see fig. 6).

Artemis, another Greek moon goddess, known in Roman mythology as Diana, was associated with hunting dogs and, according to mythology, when the chaste virgin goddess was seen by Actaeon at her bath, she angrily turned him into a stag so that he was torn to bits by his own dogs. Here we see the archetypal experience of death and dismemberment that must precede any new birth, as referred to earlier in the Isis/Osiris myth. It is interesting that Artemis' animal incarnation was the Great She Bear, Ursa Major; in this we can see the close connection between bear and dog, as noted in chapter 1 both in early religious ritual and in having evolved from a common ancestor.

According to Vedic tradition, the bitchgoddess, Sarama, was the mistress of death dogs (O'Flaherty 1975, p. 352). In ancient Babylon the fate-goddess Gula, the Great Physician

Figure 6 **Marseilles Tarot Deck**

mentioned earlier, was assimilated to Ishtar whose sacred king, Tammuz, was also torn to pieces by dogs (Walker 1983, p. 241). In Celtic mythology the Hounds of Annwn were known as the Hounds of Hell (ibid.). In the *Prose Edda*, compiled in the thirteenth century A.D., the Goddess Hel was the ruler of the land of death and gave birth to lunar wolf dogs who ate the flesh of the dead and carried souls to paradise. It was her dog Garm who was chained at the gates of the underworld. In some cultures dead bodies are actually set out for dogs to devour (Davis 1970, p. 300). Madam Pele, the Goddess of the Volcano in Hawaiian mythology, has a white dog as a companion (Knipe 1982, p. 115). This white dog is also the guardian of the Wiapio Valley, the sacred valley of the Hawaiians where king Kamehameha was sheltered during his youth. Loki, an old Hawaiian

Figure 7 **Anubis with Maat,
Weighing the Souls of the Dead**

woman whom I met quite by chance by going into an antique shop to get out of the rain, told me stories of people who had seen the white dog stalking near a volcanic crater or sitting on the rock near the entrance to the Wiapio Valley.

THE DOG AND ITS CONNECTION WITH DEATH AND REBIRTH

The jackal-headed god of Egyptian mythology who presided over the embalming process and sat at the side of Maat at the time of the decision of justice was Anubis (see fig. 7). With Anubis' assistance in helping Isis recover the body of Osiris, we can see the double meaning of the symbol, the dog/jackal as death and also recollection or rebirth. A description of a procession of Isis reveals the following to us about Anubis:

> *First to appear were women dressed in white clothes and garlands, some sprinkled the pathways with herbs and balm while others carried mirrors and ivory combs. Next came men to light the way*

Figure 8 **Roman Sculpture Relief on Marble
Sarcophagus, Second Century** A.D.

*with lamps and torches and candles. Priests and leaders came with
white surplices and bearing relics and small shrines. Finally behind
towered the gods themselves. Towering above them all was the figure
of Anubis, messenger of the gods, supernal and infernal, his dog's
head and neck rearing on high displaying alternately a face black as
night and one golden as day. He bore the caduceus in his left hand
and in his right waved a green palm branch aloft. (Dale-Green 1966,
p. 112)*

Jung suggests that the deeper meaning of the dog related to
death: that it is at the moment of death that we re-enter the
womb of the Great Mother for renewal and rebirth into the next
phase of our soul's journey. The dog as a companion to the
Great Mother provides an excellent symbol for this event. This
would explain the dog that is shown in ancient pictures leaping
upon the bull killed by Mithros as an indication that this sacrifice is also the moment of extreme fruitfulness (Jung 1956, par.
354). Jung's theory would also explain a passage in Petronius:
"I earnestly beseech you to paint a small dog around the foot of
my statue so that by kindness I may attain to life after death"
(ibid. par. 355). (See fig. 8.) It is in this role that the dog is also

associated to Asclepius. The dog who heals itself by licking itself—the notion of curing an illness—carries with it the concept of birth from death, which I feel touches on the primitive rituals of dogs sacrificed to carry messages to the gods. This is the dog in its role as psychopomp, or conductor of souls. In this role the dog is associated to Hermes, the Greek messenger god of the crossroads, as well as to Anubis, who was worshiped in Egypt and ascended into heaven in the form of Sirus the Great Dog (Walker 1983, p. 242).

When the Greeks arrived in Egypt, they were so impressed with the deities there that their gods became assimilated. Hermes was soon identified with Anubis, who in turn gave rise to Hermanubis, the dog-god of Alexandria. In the Gnostic system, it was Hermanubis who guided souls on their way through the planets to paradise (Dale-Green 1966, p. 95). Saint Christopher, the patron saint of travelers, is pictured in the Greek Orthodox Church with a head of a dog (see fig. 9). *The Menaian*, or book of Calendar Feasts, states that St. Christopher was a descendant of the Cynocephali, a legendary race of giants with human bodies and dog's heads. In western Christianity the legend developed that St. Christopher carried the Christ Child across a stream and then was changed from his part-dog form into a handsome man. In the Greek Orthodox tradition, he attempted to change an evil pagan king who imprisoned him and ordered him chained to an iron throne under which a fire was built. As the chair became hot, St. Christopher was transformed and received the face of a handsome man (Leach 1961, p. 201). There is in a Rumanian monastery at Neamtz a woodcut showing a saint with a dog's head.

In keeping with the dog and its close ties to death are the danced imitations of the dog performed in funeral and war dances. In the mourning rituals of the ancient Aztecs, a dancer impersonated the old coyote Haehuecoytl, who presided over the ceremonies. Artist George Catlin described and illustrated the exotic "dog dance" of the Sioux Indians, a dance in honor of war where dogs were eaten as part of the ceremony (Lansdale 1981, pp. 130–31).

Figure 9 **Greek Orthodox
Rendering of Saint
Christopher**

Wolf Mother

The myths of heroes being raised by wolves suggest another possibility of the connection between humans and dogs: rather than humans initiating the first gesture toward the animal, perhaps it was the animal who made the first connection to humans. As stated earlier, in ancient times there often were not separate words for dog and wolf, so myths about the wolf mother round out the association of the dog to the Goddess. The Great Goddess herself was referred to as a wolf and there

Figure 10 **The Benevolent Wolf Mother with Romulus and Remus**

was the Roman cult of the She-Wolf Lupa. It was the She-Wolf who was turned into Hecate, of the Homeric legend. There are many lupine foster mothers in mythology. It was a wolf that is said to have suckled the founders of Rome (see fig. 10). In one form of another myth, Asclepius was suckled by a wolf after being abandoned by Coronis. TuKueh, legendary founder of the Turkish nation, was preserved in infancy by a holy she-wolf, perhaps explaining why in early times dogs were revered in Turkey. Zoroaster was raised by a she-wolf and Siegfried, of Norse mythology, was also a wolf's foster child, his oldest name being Wolf Dietrich (Walker 1983, p. 243). Galahad, of the King Arthur legends, was carried to safety by Merlin in the form of a wolf (Luke 1975, p. 19). These myths show the life-giving quality of the dog/wolf. The hero, which is new consciousness, is nourished by connection to the Great Mother. This idea is still alive, as can be seen from the following quotation from a family journal (the birthdate of the child Hannible was 1842, according to court records):

> *Somewhere in the North Carolina mountains Hannible was playing while his mother was washing clothes. He was about 3 or 4 years old at the time. A man rode by on a white horse and Hannible's parents believe the man picked Hannible up and carried him up the mountain because the man was mad at Hannible's father. Hannible was gone 3 days and nights and said he slept with a mother dog and her pups. His parents believe they must have been wolves. Hannible said he ate and drank with the dogs. When they went to get a drink he fell in the water and the mother dog pulled him out by his clothes. His clothes were torn when his parents found him asleep under some low hanging rocks. Hannible said the mother dog brought him raw meat but he could not eat it. When he tried to climb up after berries growing on a bush, the mother dog gnawed it down and brought it to him.*[5]

This double image of the dog as accompanier of the soul in death as well as the accompanier of new birth gives the dog the exemplary position of guide, or psychopomp, to new beginnings.

Notes

1. In early times there was no word to differentiate wolf from dog, and there is in fact a great difference between the two, as illustrated by this fable from Aesop.

The Dog and the Wolf
Discouraged after an unsuccessful day of hunting, a hungry wolf came on a well-fed mastiff. He could see that the dog was having a better time of it than he was and he inquired what the dog had to do to stay so well fed. "Very little," said the dog. "Just drive away beggars, guard the house, show fondness to the master, be submissive to the rest of the family and you are well fed and warmly lodged."

The wolf thought this over carefully. He risked his own life almost daily, had to stay out in the worst of weather, and was never assured of his meals. He thought he would try another way of living.

As they were going along together, the wolf saw a place around the dog's neck where the hair had worn thin. He asked what this was and the dog said it was nothing—"Just the place where my collar and chain rub." The wolf stopped short, "Chain?" He asked. "You mean you are not free to go where you choose?" "No," said the dog, "but what does that mean?" "Much," answered the wolf as he trotted off. "Much."

2. Nut's rightful spouse Ra had cursed her when he discovered her union with Seb and decreed that she could not deliver in year or month, which meant she could only deliver on a day not in the solar calendar. Through trickery, Thoth, who also loved Nut, was able to add the five days to the solar year.

3. More will be said of the role of Anubis under the section on the death and rebirth aspect of the archetype.

4. This leads to an interesting view of individuation. It is my personal belief, and von Franz is here suggesting this, that individuation—the process by which we become wholly ourselves, distinct from others and yet paradoxically related to others—is a natural unfolding that has its roots in the deepest layers of the psyche, the psychoid unconscious. This most fundamental level of the unconscious has properties in common with the organic world and is neither wholly psychological nor wholly physiological. The archetype as applied to the psychoid unconscious is depicted by Jung as a spectrum ranging from an "infra-red," or physiological and instinctual pole, to the "ultra-violet," or spiritual, imaginal pole, and is the psychic-organic or mind-body connection. The Jungian view of individuation includes the natural process but it also includes reflection upon the experience so that it becomes conscious. Charles Williams (1974, p. 144) understood this very well when he wrote, "Flesh knows what spirit knows, but spirit knows it knows."

5. I am deeply indebted to June Bratcher of Raleigh, N.C., who shared this quotation from her family journal.

Chapter 4

Dreams and Sandtray Analysis

> I love inseeing. Can you imagine with me
> how glorious it is to insee, for example, a dog
> as one passes by. To insee (I don't mean
> inspect, which is only a kind of human gym-
> nastic, by means of which one immediately
> comes out again on the other side of the dog,
> regarding it merely, so to speak, as a window
> upon the humanity lying behind it, not that) —
> but to let oneself precisely into the dog, the
> place in it where God, as it were, would have
> sat down for a moment when the dog was
> finished, in order to watch it under the influ-
> ence of its first embarrassments and inspira-
> tions and to know that it was good that noth-
> ing was lacking, that it could not have been
> better made. . . . Laugh though you may,
> dear confidant, if I am to tell you where my
> all-greatest feeling, my world-feeling, my
> earthly bliss was to be found, I must confess
> to you: it was to be found time and again,
> here and there, in such timeless moments of
> this divine inseeing.
>
> *Rainer Maria Rilke*

The previous chapter touched on some of the basic archetypal aspects of the symbol of the dog. There is an enor-
mous amount of mythological material about the dog because
the dog has been so closely associated with humankind over
such a long period. This discussion has focused on the nature
of the human-dog bond and has been limited to viewing the
dog as a helpful animal and the dog in relation to life and
death, the soul guide.

Now in this chapter I will present the dreams of analysands

which actually stirred my interest and curiosity and led me to write this book. Some of the dreams were specifically of my dog Tinsel; others were of dogs unknown to me, but the dreamer would associate the dog to Tinsel. In addition, I have also included a dream of a dear friend who has allowed me to use her dream because it so beautifully represents the motif of the dog and its association to the feminine, instinctual wisdom of nature, which is being in the moment and knowing in that moment what is right and what is wrong. I will also discuss a sandtray as an example of a specific aspect of the archetype. Some of the content of the dreams will clearly involve transference and countertransference—or the feelings that my analysands have about me, and vice versa, and the projections each of us makes onto the other—but beyond this there is more to be found in the symbol of the dog.

DREAM ONE

The first dream I will discuss comes from Jim who was 38 years old when he began therapy. He came at the suggestion of his fiancée, who was concerned about his episodes of rage, followed by isolation and withdrawal. This dream came after we had been working together about three years and turned out to be pivotal in his life.

Dream 1: I was walking alone along a dark road in a wooded place. I am in a hurry although I don't know where I am or where I am going. Suddenly a small dog comes along and begins to nip at my heels. It is as if he wants me to stop, maybe even to play with him, but I am in a hurry and I kick him hard to shake him loose. I am so angry that I kicked him very hard so that he is maybe hurt and I see him lying at the side of the road.

This dream made a big impact on this man, and, although he faithfully recorded dreams and made copies of them to bring me, often several for each session, his dreams did not consciously seem to have any effect on changing his behavior. With this dream, however, he was very sad and on the one hand could own his extreme anger when he was interrupted or did not feel in control, but on the other hand he could also feel a real sadness and loss over having hurt the dog. He associated the dog nipping at his heel to the little nippers in his classroom. He is a teacher of learning disabled children in an inner city school, and often in our discussion referred to his students as "little nippers." He admits feeling overwhelmed with the neediness of these children and has often reacted to it with a punitive inner rage that has created a great deal of guilt in himself.

Jim is a son of a naval commander who wanted to run his home like a ship. The father physically abused him, the mother, and the younger brother in order to maintain control. Allowing him to give expression to his reactions to such abuse as well as helping him see how he had internalized his father as part of his own identity was the core of our early work together. To be isolated, angry, distrustful, unable to maintain any type of relationship had been his usual pattern of existence. He was always suspicious of having Tinsel in the office and was able to tell me that he did not like her and that he was afraid she would attack him if he would express his anger with me. He normally ignored her when she would walk out to greet him, but she showed no particular anxiety about his behavior and would usually lie quietly in the office, either behind his chair or behind my chair.

Jim is ego intact and was able to discuss this material. He was aware that the violence he feared from Tinsel was his own, as she was never in any way aggressive toward him. He understood the dream on two levels. First, objectively, the dog represented me, the analyst who nipped at his heels to help guide him through the dark woods, which he felt was his own state of angry depression. Jim, as you can suspect, was most difficult to work with because no matter what intervention I would try to make, I was met with anger. He would accuse me of either not empathizing enough with him or of taking his experiences too seriously and feeling he was hopeless. He interpreted my attempts to help him understand why relationships with others were not working as meaning I was not appreciating him. He was able to see in this dream at this level how he kicked my interventions aside. At the second level, the subjective level, he came to see the little nippers in his class as his own wounded child. He, in turn, behaved like his father with aggression and anger toward any felt weakness or any lack of control. He could feel as himself the little dog who had been kicked aside. He had seen his brother being kicked by his father in anger. He could see how he kicked the child part of himself that wants to play, that wants to be recognized and be part of him. It had taken three years of treatment in a safe, non-retaliatory space for the child part of him to even begin to show itself, and in this case it appeared first with the help of, and in the form of, a dog.[1]

The fact that this dream had such an emotional effect on him attests to its coming during a transition or growth period in his psyche. He has referred to this dream many times as we continued to work on his awareness of his own inner child and that part of his psyche's need for play. He learned that he has the ability to respond to his own needs so as to not expect needs to be met always from the outside, with the subsequent disappointment and anger when it doesn't happen. He made a decision after this dream to make friends with Tinsel, and he began initiating friendly overtures when she walked out to greet him. His pleasure was very apparent when she would wag her tail or put her head in his lap to be petted. I am not going to say that the dream effected a miraculous healing because he continues to work hard and changes are slow, but the dream clearly came at a time when he was ready to understand and respond. The image of the dark wood in which he walked is almost classical in representing the place of the *nigredo,* the dark night of the soul, the beginning place of a step toward growth. Dante begins his *Inferno* with, "Midway this way of life we're bound upon I woke to find myself in a dark wood, where the right road was wholly lost and gone" (Sayers 1951, p. 71). Dante found his guides in Virgil and Beatrice, whereas Jim, who is on this journey, finds his companion in me, in my dog, and at a deeper level in this child side of himself or deeper instinctive side as represented by the dog.

The dream image is very similar to the image on the tarot card, the Fool discussed at length in chapter 3. The dog in the dream is nipping at his heels much as the dog on many Fool cards is shown nipping at the jester's heels. It might appear that the dog is trying to hurt him, but this is not the case. Barbara Hannah (1953–54, Lecture 3, p. 7) in her lectures at the

C. G. Jung Institute in Küsnacht, Switzerland, talked about the dog as representing the deepest and most primitive level of instinct. She stated that the dog was often depicted in myths as a troublemaker because the instincts have to betray us or make themselves known in some way for consciousness to develop. The dog instinct, as she describes it, is that deep instinct to do what is just right, at the moment. She also stated that the instinct as represented by the dog can be integrated. (There are motifs and fairy tales where the dog actually becomes human.) Although the dream of my analysand contained the figure of a dog, as he talked more and more about the dream, he would interchange the word "child" for "dog." The changes in his attitudes and consequently in his life showed he was ready to integrate the meaning of the dream.

DREAM TWO

The second dream is that of Lisa, a 38-year-old married woman with two children. She is an extremely sensitive and gifted woman, born into a family with a cold, perfectionistic, uncompromising mother and a father who is highly successful and almost unscrupulous, who defends his questionable ethics by fundamentalist religiosity. In her early years she had a dog who was her "best friend," and there is a family dog in her present home that is primarily hers. From the very beginning of our work together she enjoyed having Tinsel in the office, and Tinsel would respond to her in very special ways. Although this woman came into analysis because of a "vague sense of emptiness" and some questions about her direction in her chosen profession, she soon began to be able to move toward the profound depression of her childhood which she had been able to keep repressed through most of her adult years. During this time she would often sob throughout an entire session, sometimes sitting in a chair and at other times preferring to sit on the floor. Tinsel would often put her head into Lisa's lap, sometimes whimpering, or at other times she would just lie alongside her on the floor with her head across Lisa's knee, thereby giving her a great deal of comfort. During this period, when Lisa had been in therapy about a year and was beginning to allow herself to feel her depression, she had the following dream:

Dream 2: I am all alone in a very dark place crying. I am small and very afraid. I feel so bad that I think about committing suicide. Then a dog comes and begins to lick my tears and I know I will be all right.

Her associations to this dream were the remembrance of how lonely she had felt as a child and her memory of thinking about suicide when she was about seven years old. She first associated the dog in the dream to Tinsel and then to me, and it is clear that Tinsel was an extension of me in the transference experience where she feels in a safe and accepting relationship. On an inner level the dog who comes to her verifies my own sense of the deep instinctive resources that were available to this woman in her healing process. The experience of being in the deepest blackness of death, her thought of suicide, is connected with the image of the dog as discussed in chapter 3, that is, the dog carrying within it the double aspect of life and death. In Greek mythology, Cerberus was said to have never seen light, but Hercules' twelfth task was to bring Cerberus up from the underworld and, when Cerberus saw the light, he sneezed, and at this spot foxglove grew. Digitalis, derived from foxglove, is poison but is also used as medication for heart problems, so this myth like many others illustrates the connection between dog, death, healing, and the heart (Hannah 1953–54, Lecture 5, p. 1). I emphasized the relationship between the dog's instincts and the heart because, as the alchemists knew, knowledge and learning can go only so far and there is a point when the alchemists advise, "tear up your books so that you hearts be not torn asunder" (ibid., Lecture 4, p. 8). In short, in individuation, true knowledge comes only from the heart, and an animal with a loving heart, such as a dog, can guide us in these places. The image of the dog licking Lisa's tears is also most important. The analysand felt this dream to be very healing and reassuring and that she would indeed make it through her depression.

The dog is an agent of healing, as already discussed in the cult of Asclepius in chapter 3. The inscription at the temple of

Epidaurus that says "one of the sacred dogs took care with its tongue of a child who had a tumor on its head" is relevant to this dream. The dog heals itself by licking itself. It is in the act of licking that healing lies. Spittle is soul substance, a psychic substance or essence. Jung learned of this from the sun worship of the Elgonyi, from an old medicine man of a Masai village. Each morning when the sun appeared in the sky, the people stepped out in front of their huts, spat on their hands, and held them up to the sun. Since to the primitive mind spittle is a substance of life and soul, their gesture means: "I offer God my living Soul" (Jung 1979, p. 166). Spittle, according to primitive belief, contained the personal manna, the life force, the power to heal and the power to make magic (Jung 1964, par. 146). In this light when the dog licks us, it is really massaging us with the essence of its soul. Certain Indians believe that dogs are actually killed for their tongue, which contains a healing ambrosia. There is a French proverb that states "the tongue of a dog can be used for medicine" (as quoted in Hannah 1953-54, Lecture 5, p. 4). The dog licking her tears was indeed healing for Lisa, for although she had to experience a deep sense of depression as we uncovered the pain of her early childhood, she gained a sense that she could work through this, which indeed she continues to do.

DREAM THREE

Frances is a 46-year-old woman whom I have been seeing for about five years. This dream came at a time of transition in her development when she was ready to begin healing a deep and chronic depression. She is a very intelligent and creative woman who suffered early emotional abuse, causing her to give up her own identity and any attempt to express her own feelings or ideas to become her parents' "doll" and live out their unfulfilled lives. Because she was living far below her natural potential in her adult life, she felt a deep sense of emptiness and insecurity. Pets had not been part of her early life, but she enjoyed Tinsel's attention and was deeply touched when Tinsel would come and stand beside her or put her head into her lap when she was crying.

Dream 3: I am walking in a deep dark woods. I don't know where I am going. A large dark dog appears. It acts as if I am to follow it, as if it will lead me through these woods. I am very afraid of the dog and do not want to follow. An old hermit who lives in the woods comes and tells me that the dog will help. When I see the hermit is really Jesus, I know that it will be all right and begin to follow.

Her associations to this dream were that the dark woods were the confusion and chaos that she had felt inside herself most of her life. A wooded area was both exciting and frightening to her for fear of getting lost. She associated Tinsel to the dog both in her friendly way of being and also in what she felt was something frightening about her because of the unknown, sort of the "uncanny" way in which Tinsel behaved. I believe that Frances in this dream has touched upon the paradox of the symbol of the dog as guide by her fear of the dog. This points to her inner knowledge of the dog as guide to the other world, as with both Anubis and Hermes. It could take her deeper and deeper into blackness, so that in a sense fear is an appropriate response. Anubis is often represented as double-natured— Anubis lying down and Upuant standing up. Upuant means "opener of the ways," and in certain writings becomes identical with Hermes, the messenger, or Mercury. The dog in Frances's dream was standing up. In Greek mythology Hermes wears the kynee, a helmet or cap shaped in the likeness of the dog's head. The idea that the dog takes us to the next world is part of the religious ritual of sacrifice of the dog, as already discussed in chapter 1. In primitive groups in North Asia and currently by some Native American tribes, the dog is sacrificed to conduct the soul or to send prayers to the creator. Whereas the dog can be seen as guide to the upper world, Frances instinctively knew that the dog was also the guardian of Hell and companion of Hecate, the dark goddess. She was ready to meet the aspects of the dark goddess within herself, to confront the depth of her own rage, and to emerge with a greater sense of her own power as a woman. The dog indeed was her proper companion.

Frances has suffered a great deal because she had not been listening to her own instincts. Her natural passion had been projected out onto men in relationships that have been unrewarding and destructive. With the dog as her companion and guide to her instinctual psyche, she has begun to accept and be in touch with her passion as her own. This she experiences as a new sense of joy in life. I feel it is important to note that it was the hermit whom she recognized as Jesus who told her it was safe to accompany the dog. At one level, this may be seen as her still being dependent on the masculine to instruct her course, a woman who continues to be a father's daughter in her inner life, a woman who looks to the patriarchy for authority. Frances is indeed a father's daughter, but she is coming to the positive side of the complex; she is finding a deep spiritual connection to the masculine within her. The meaning of the woman and her dog is an important image for Frances. It is an image that I will discuss more completely in chapter 5.

Frances had another dog dream about one year later. It was a dream about a three-legged dog that was otherwise healthy and strong and finding its way confidently through the streets of a city. As we talked about the dream, she felt distressed at first that the dog had only three legs. But as she discussed this dream more fully, she remembered the details of the dream in which the dog seemed healthy, happy, and competent. With a sudden awareness she realized that she was like the three-legged dog. She had been deeply affected, in a way crippled, by her experiences in early life. But individuation, the task of consciously accepting all that we are so that we come to wholeness, does not mean perfection. Her life could have meaning when she could see that all of her life experiences and all of her feelings led her to be uniquely herself. She was capable and could be happy simply being herself. As she could see the meaning in her life, she was able to forgive herself for not being perfect. She could genuinely mourn her lost childhood, become more independent, and relate to her parents as an adult rather than as their "doll." At this point she could also feel some forgiveness for her parents and see them in the light of their own life experiences. It was shortly after this dream that she knew she had completed her analysis. When our life has meaning, we are able to come into a state of peace with

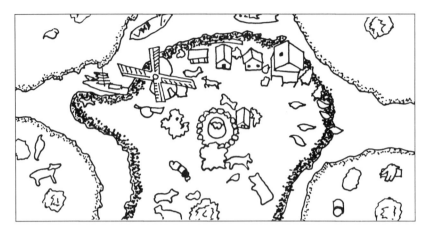

Figure 11 **Reconstituted Sandtray**

ourselves and with others. It was this task that Frances, with the dog as her guide, was able to accomplish.

SANDTRAY ANALYSIS

An example of the dog in its role of instincts in terms of protective guard of the deep inner self appeared in a sandtray of an adolescent girl who had just been removed from her father's custody after two instances of his molesting two of her friends. I was made aware of this sandtray by a very good friend who is a sandtray therapist; in this tray the entire center of the tray looks like a dog's head in profile (see fig. 11). In figure 12 there is a second dog in front of a house directly to the right of the central crystal. The analysand stated in discussing the tray that "the jewel was brought from the sea and the crystal made a wall around the jewel. The animals present have powers that protect and guard the land." The jewel is clearly a symbol of the Self, that central unifying part of the psyche analogous to the life spark, or that part that is open to images of God. Jung has used the term Self to express the center and totality of the personality embracing all consciousness and the unconscious. This center of being, this central mystery of life, has a thousand names, such as Buddha in Buddhism, the Brahmin in Hinduism, Christ in Christianity, the stone in alchemy, the diamond,

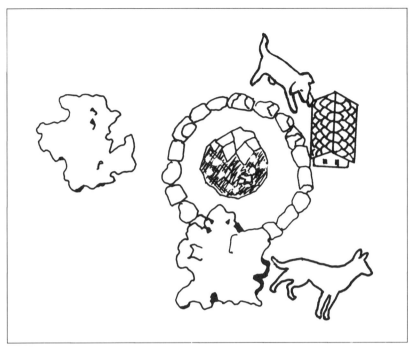

Figure 12 **Reconstituted Sandtray**

the child, the flower, the circle, the square, the Tao in China. In this tray the dog that is directly next to the jewel's outer circle represents, I believe, the instinctive trustworthy energy that guards and protects us.

DREAMS FOUR AND FIVE

I would like now to discuss two dreams of two different analysands, where the dog aids new life, that is, a motif of entrusting a child—the new growth—into the care of the instinctive feminine. This is the image in which a baby is entrusted to the care of a dog, as in the myth of Romulus and Remus. I have commented already on the closeness of the symbol of the dog to the feminine principle—both in the concept of the Fool card of the tarot deck and in the association of the dog with the goddess. Although both dreams 4 and 5 have a clearly transferential component, they also speak to something deeper in the psyche.

Dream 4 comes from Louise, a 38-year-old woman with whom I worked for about four years. She is married, has children, and is successful professionally but has suffered episodes of deep depression and had been in treatment for several years before beginning her work with me. Because of her own intelligence and strength she has been able to move beyond her most difficult childhood. Her mother was overtly psychotic, emotionally abusive to her, and undermining of her; her father was very strict, requiring that his rigid code of behavior be enforced by severe physical punishment. The cost to her has been an inner rage that she has felt as overwhelming depression with feelings of worthlessness, ideas of suicide, isolation, and a marked distrust of others. Louise did not have a pet as a child, but she does have a dog in her home now, and she has at times felt this was her only friend. She has enjoyed Tinsel even at times when she has expressed rage and anger toward me. The fact that she could like my dog while hating me is an example of the kind of splitting defense which she has used to maintain herself. It was also a clue to me of the potential for healing in Louise. This is her dream:

Dream 4: I see Tinsel lying on the floor. I take my small child and place her against Tinsel in the middle so that she is safe and contained there.

There was a great deal of feeling associated to this dream and her immediate associations to it were her feelings about me. She was able to express the irrationality of the degree of anger that she felt toward me and was able to talk about her ambivalent feelings of both liking me and being afraid of trusting me for fear that she would be rejected and abandoned. This dream seemed to be a turning point in her ability to bring good and bad feelings together and to be able to trust that she could be safe and contained in the therapeutic relationship. At a deeper level it is a new view of the possibility of a positive relationship to the feminine through the experience of the caring She-dog. I believe this dream is indicating the movement that is taking place in her psyche: she is beginning to see the possibility of a positive feminine within herself, even though at this point it is represented in the form of a dog.

The second dream of this type was dreamed by Betsy, a woman of 34 whom I have been seeing for about three years. This woman too, though married and with children and a successful profession, is deeply wounded in her connection to the feminine side of herself and suffers severe depressions, with suicidal thoughts. She has had extensive psychotherapy, with medication prescribed in the past because of her depression. This dream occurred very early in her treatment, reflecting her psychic readiness to begin the treatment process. She had not had a pet in her early life but enjoyed Tinsel's presence in my office.

Dream 5: I am driving in a car with my baby. The car is stalled but a German Shepherd dog comes and takes the baby from the car to care for it. The baby will be all right.

As is typical of Betsy, she was unable to give any detailed associations at all to the dream but she associated a sense of peace to it and has referred to the dream many times in the course of our continuing work. My own sense is that it showed a feeling of potential for trust in the therapeutic relationship, but because of the degree of woundedness and the fact that she still had much unconscious material to deal with, her trust was expressed in the symbol of the dog. Betsy has stayed with the analytic process in spite of the long hard work of dealing with her resistance to facing her own feelings. She was the oldest of six children, born into a very limited, overtly religious, rural family, where basic survival took the energy of both of her parents, and there was little in the way of felt emotional support. Her car, which is her energy and way of going, indeed has been stalled in that she has been stuck in pretending to be all right, a reaction formation to her own sense of worthlessness. This has prevented her from being able to truly align with her own energy and assimilate her experience as her own essential part of who she is as an individual. But she continues to work, and I feel the prognosis is favorable because the baby is safe and being cared for by the deep instincts within.

DREAM SIX

The last dream I want to include in this chapter is not from an analysand but from a very dear woman friend. I include it because it so beautifully puts into imagery what can be difficult to put into words regarding the dog as an image of our deepest instincts. Further it represents the relationship among the ego, the dreamer, and the instinctual nature within, as represented by the dog. This harmonious relationship between ego and instincts is the movement and the goal as the individuated personality grows into maturity.

Dream 6: I am watching a pack of dogs, a leader and four smaller dogs. The leader is also the mother of them all, steady and wise. The oldest of the others is my own dog. The mother's coat is a pale gold color with a sort of numinous shining quality. She is perhaps a mixture of Shepherd, Collie, and Golden Retriever. They move swiftly and quietly over all sorts of terrain, including city streets full of traffic. I am fearful for them on the streets, but see how surely and safely the leader takes them through the traffic. I have a glimpse of them out in the sandy country and see the leader pause at a hole; she is teaching the others to hunt now. When she senses the younger ones are tired, she seeks out a safe spot and all sit down and rest before going on their way again. Now they are near the ocean, and I see to my distress that the youngest and smallest has fallen into a pool and the leader has not noticed. I run and lift her out and think desperately she should have artificial respiration and I have not the skill, and I start running, calling for a man who has an artificial respiration clinic. Meanwhile I press on the dog's ribs. A little water comes out, she gives a cough and starts to breathe naturally. The artificial respiration man hints that after drowning, a *painful* treatment in his parlor is essential. I wonder if I should have given the dog to his ministrations but am sure that nature has done all the healing necessary. I put her down and she happily joins the others who are waiting for her. The leader serenely takes them off to a spot beside a house so that the little one may rest and recover, I think. A few people are watching. Some seem to have known the leader for a long time. A man says to me, "She has new younger dogs with her since I saw her last." I am worrying again. Will they get home safely through all the traffic, and should I take my dog with me now? Then I remember the extraordinary poise and awareness of the mother-leader and know it would be all wrong away from this, her natural place. What risks there are must be taken. Friends drive up at this point and I join them in a car, looking back as we drive off, for I am reluctant to leave the extraordinary beauty of the resting animals. They have an aloofness, a feeling of fulfilling their natural instincts, guided by the quiet maturity of the older dog, and of going their own way utterly undeterred by all the modern mechanical noise, or the fussing of human beings.

This profoundly moving dream conveys a deep sense of peace in the purity of the instincts. This quality comes from the image of the dog within us fulfilling its own nature in the very heart of the mechanized world. The dream states that vigilance is needed, not to protect the dogs from the activity of the modern world but in case the "little one" should wander off and fall into the unconscious. The dream tells us how to deal with moments of unconsciousness, represented in the dream as the smallest dog falling into the pool. When we make a mistake, most of us are beset by guilt, which results in an inner attack of self-criticism. This is the painful treatment that we impose on ourselves, and it affects our self-confidence and relationship to others. The dream says that all that is really needed is just a simple squeeze, a moment of reflection to allow consciousness to occur, and life will be able to go on in a natural way. In the dream the dog gives a cough and starts to breathe normally

Figure 13 **Reconstituted Sandtray**

again. The passage bridging the mind and body is cleared and life can continue in its wholeness.

I have presented this dream in detail because it so beautifully depicts the dog within us, the instincts in their relationship to the feminine and to the natural movement of meeting and attending to each moment.

These dreams that I have discussed here are but a few of the many dreams that have been brought to me. They are the dreams that inspired me to look further into the meaning of the symbol of the dog and the dog's relationship to humankind. I will close this chapter now with a picture of a sandtray (see fig. 13) which I did in Switzerland several years ago, where I had gone to meet with Dora Kalff, who developed the therapeutic use of the sandtray for working with analysands, to learn more about the technique for my own practice.

I made the tray in figure 13 before I had conceived of the idea of writing about the human-dog bond, but it shows how closely linked the symbol of the dog is with the central essence of my own psyche and why having a dog in my office and writing about the dog is a natural unfolding of my own process of individuation.

Note

1. Harold Searls (1960, pp. 261–68) discusses dream material from his patients to suggest that the form of an animal may be an unconscious conception of self in a non-human form, which may be the beginnings of the recovering of self-esteem.

Chapter 5

A Jungian View of the Human-Dog Bond

> If I were alone in a desert where I was afraid,
> and if I had a child with me, my fear would
> disappear and I would be strengthened; so
> noble, so full of pleasure, and so powerful is
> life in itself. If I could not keep a child with
> me and if I had at least a live animal with me,
> I would be comforted. Therefore, let those
> who bring about great wonders in black books
> take an animal, perhaps a dog, to help them.
> The life within the animal will give them
> strength. Equality gives strength in all things.
> *Meister Eckhart*

In my attempt to understand more about the human-dog bond by looking at some of the archetypal aspects of the dog through the grid of mythology and the dreams of some of my analysands, it was important to start with the history of the dog's relationship to humans. There was a need for early people to identify with the forces of nature: animals, trees, water, mountains, wind, and stars. Then as the powers of abstraction and consciousness developed, these forces became part of human ritual and mythology. The cave bear and the dog, being in some ways like early humans, carried the projections of the unknown, which was felt within man. These animals then became part of religious ritual, with worshiping and the offering of gifts to these animals and then the sacrificing of the animals themselves in place of human sacrifices. As long as primitive humans continued to associate with nature, frightened as they may have been they did not feel alienated either from themselves or from the universe. Dogs in this sense mediated between the known terrors in outer reality and the unknown terrors of the inner world. This very early use of the dog was carried in the mythologies of various cultures, but the mythologies gradually changed in form as they were influenced by the progress in the cultures themselves. The very nature of the dog—its tendency to live in groups, its willingness to bond and give loyalty to another, its natural willingness to guard—gave it the special status of being the first animal to share its life with human beings. This has placed the dog closest to humans, but it also provided the closest link to the nonhuman or other world. The dog has been the guide par excellence in this world, and in some early cultures, as I discussed in chapter 3, dogs were associated with the gods and goddesses in the mystery of life and death.

As populations increased and problems of sanitation and disease occurred, the fact that dogs carried disease, especially rabies, increased the dog's association with the devil, evil, and death. Just as the death aspect of the Great Goddess was split off from her other energies, so the death aspect of the dog was split off from the other aspect of the dog as guide and it began to take on more negative associations. Even by the time of late Greek culture, the dog began to be so despised that the snake remained in the company of Asclepius in the form of the caduceus, which is an emblem of the medical profession, but the dog lost its position. Although the dog had a place among the gods in older religions, by the time of the Old Testament and early Christianity it lost this position. In the Bible it was considered an "unclean" animal, with almost every reference to the dog suggesting a lowly and degraded nature. It is suggested by Henry P. Davis in his classic *The Modern Dog Encyclopedia* (1970, p. 300) that the graven images the Jews were forbidden to idolize might well have included that of Anubis, the dog-headed deity of Egypt. It may have been that because of the reverence bestowed upon the dog by the Egyptians, the Hebrews were so emphatic in declaring the dog an object of abomination. Simon Magnus, the sorcerer of the Apocrypha, sent to the apostle Peter certain devils in the likeness of dogs to devour him (Dale-Green 1966, p. 80). English folklore of the seventh century referred to the black dog Skriker, the shaggy dog form of the devil, as a forerunner of death (*Time-Life* 1985, pp. 11–17). In the seventeenth century there is a document in which Elizabeth Clark confessed to a carnal connection to the devil through her dog (Dale-Green 1966, p. 79) and James Denice confessed to being responsible for the death of four people by willing his dog to kill them (ibid.). In Goethe's *Faust* the author included material from medieval times, with Mephistopheles' first appearance being in the guise of a dog. Even now "dog" includes among its definitions in the Random House College Dictionary: "something worthless, of extremely poor quality; an ugly, boring, or crude girl or woman. *To go to the dogs* is to deteriorate, degenerate morally or physically, or to go to ruin. And *to lead a dog's life* is to have an unhappy, or harassed, existence."

At the International Symposium on the Human-Pet Relationship in Vienna in 1983, James Serpell gave a report on cross-cultural variations in attitudes toward dogs and showed that in countries where dogs are a major source of infectious disease, contact is generally prohibited by social and religious taboos. In countries where dogs are used for food or arduous tasks, there is a cultural attitude discouraging positive, affectionate contact with dogs (pp. 112–15). A personal interview with Jamal Bayati, a Muslim scholar, about the Muslim attitude to dogs revealed that there is nothing written in the Koran about the inherent evil of dogs, but because Mohammed was reported to have said when he pointed to a dog, "There goes the devil" as well as, "Anyone keeping a dog except for hunting or farming would lose a measure of good will," the religious attitude toward dogs soon incorporated these stories. Perhaps this attitude is also based on dogs carrying disease in that part of the world. However, even in the Muslim tradition the opposite attitude is also present. Javad Nurbakhsh states in *Canine Symbolism in Sufi Literature:* "Saying of Ali (Peace Be Upon Him): Happy is the person whose life resembles that of a dog's life because there are 10 manners of a dog each believer should possess" (1987, pp. 5–6).[1] In this instance the dog would be the perfect Sufi. This would further support the idea that the dog was not considered inherently evil in the Muslim world but that the negative associations developed within a changing culture.

Myths consistently show attitudes about and associations to dogs that contain both the positive and negative sides consistent with changes in the cultures that became incorporated into their mythologies. The dog then was either a sacred mediator of heaven or a symbol of the fearful mediator of death. In modern times the limit of our association to dogs and their usefulness to us is limited only by our imaginations, but our connections to dogs have a much deeper meaning than only their utilitarian use either as working dogs or as companions. Matthew Fox (1979, pp. 165–68) states that when he tells groups that his dog is his spiritual director, he is being only partly facetious. Because in our modern, mechanized world living creatures are raised like crops for food and sensitive animals capable of feeling both physical and emotional pain are subject to the most brutal and tortuous experimentation – most of which is totally unnecessary and for non-medical reasons – it is time to be conscious of what we are doing because we have some important spiritual lessons to learn from our connection to animals.

Fox suggests that animals can be happy and do not hesitate to demonstrate their joy; they can play for no reason at all and need no justification for this; they can communicate the truth in nonverbal ways using the universal language of facial expression and bodily movement; they bring beauty into our lives by their very existence, and humor by their awareness of the paradox of life in their sensing of life's contrary elements. These lessons, which he suggests we can learn from animals, are very closely connected to an aspect of the feminine principle – the deep instinctual wisdom of nature, being in the moment and knowing in that moment what is right and what is wrong. Jung himself wrote to Phylip Wylie, "People don't know that the only true servants of God are the animals. Now how are you going to bring up people to the understanding that any lousy dog is much more pious than they are?" (Jung 1975, p. xxxix).

There has been much discussion recently in Jungian psychology about the need to return to the relationship with the feminine. Edward Whitmont has written *Return of the Goddess* (1982). Nathan Schwartz-Salant has written in his book, *Narcissism and Character Transformation* (1982, pp. 133–54), that the second phase of transformation of the narcissistic personality disorder is a recovery of the feminine side of the personality. He writes about the recovery of the soul, the uniqueness, the capacity for imaginal seeing, the actively receptive, yielding side of our psyche where it is possible to be in each moment as feminine consciousness. The recovery of this aspect of the feminine is the recovery of the soul part of our psyche, which is that part of ourselves that is receptive to the images of value outside of ourselves. Ann Belford Ulanov in her book, *The Feminine in Jungian Psychology and in Christian Theology* (1971, pp. 170–74), writes about the feminine spirit as the quality of the psyche that creates unity by yielding to, embracing, and concretizing the numinous within itself, bringing spirit into the concrete happenings of everyday life.

The Sanskrit root of the word "to be" is "to grow," thus indicating the transformative aspect of feminine being. This sense of recovery of the feminine is the goddess with her dog, as she has come from the earliest of mythologies. The wisdom of the goddess carries with it the deep wisdom of connection to otherness in the form of the instinctive side of ourselves. The image of the goddess and her dog had great meaning in early times, connecting the goddess in her role of earth mother to all aspects of life, including death, which in turn contains within it the possibility of new life. The dog was the instinctive guide in these realms. Jung concluded from his study of alchemy that the dog was a symbol of the transformational agent that changed instinct into spirit and, at the moment of death, contained the element of rebirth. Just as the concept of death and rebirth reflects the bipolar eternal process of change, so the goddess with the dog reflects that part of the feminine aspect of the psyche that can be in each moment, receive, and respond in just the right way for that moment by the process of taking what is received and joining it with the richness of the instinctive level of the unconscious. This is a response that does not come from the ego level of the psyche but contains within it the natural forces from the archetypal source.

Jung was the first of the modern psychologists to understand the feminine as an archetype inherent in the psyche of both men and women. As we attempt to reacquaint ourselves with parts of the feminine, that is, with the receptive state of "being," we are also returning to the goddess and her dog as connection to the instincts. Just as dogs are civilized, so too can the instincts be civilized and balanced by the development of human consciousness that allows for the human capacity for choice. For modern men and women instincts symbolized by the dog are especially valuable since the dog has the power of the wolf. But, because of its willingness to bond, the instinctive energy is at the disposal of the conscious ego. Men and women cannot confront the archetypal world alone but the ego can safely deal with these deeper layers of the psyche when accompanied by the dog, as is clear from the case material I presented in chapter 4. It is connection to these instincts that Marie-Louise von Franz (1970, pp. xiii–4) stated propel us toward further development, and with the dog as guide these instincts can be met. Marion Woodman has written that "without the experience of instincts, the psyche is not embodied" (1985, p. 29). Wholeness must include the physical as well as the psychical.

The drawings of Anubis sitting with Maat at the time of justice show Anubis looking to the right, toward consciousness (Walker 1984) (see fig. 7). The very strength of our civilization is based on a quality of life marked by the relationship of the conscious to the unconscious and by the relationship of mutuality between human and animal. Albert Schweitzer has stated: "The great fault of all ethics hitherto has been that they believe themselves to have to deal only with the relations of man to man. In reality, however, the question is his attitude to the world and all life that comes within his reach. A man is ethical only when life as such is sacred to him, that of plants and animals as well as that of his fellow man" (1953, p. 126). This is similar to the statement Chief Seattle made in 1855, quoted at the beginning of chapter 1. "What is man without beasts? If all the beasts are gone, man would die from great loneliness of spirit, for whatever happens to beasts also happens to man. All things are connected. Whatever befalls the earth befalls the sons of the earth" (Fogel 1981, p. 334). This is the attitude of the feminine principle. It is with this attitude that we can return to the meaning of the goddess.

I suggest in this book that the archetypal core of human-kind's relationship to dogs comes from our instinctive religious need for kinship to nature because of the awareness that we are alone and yet are united to all things. And it is the feminine principle in the psyche of both men and women that allows the human-dog bond to develop. Larry Dossey, M.D., in his book *Space, Time and Medicine* (1982, pp. 72–75), states that the "thousands of individual carbon, hydrogen, and oxygen atoms that comprise our genes are in constant exchange with the world outside and like the many elements in the earth's crust they have cycled through a lifetime of several stars before eventually finding their way into our bodies." In fact, our roots go deep; he says, "We are anchored in the stars" (ibid., pp. 72–75). The etymology of the work "disaster" comes from the Latin word *disastrum* and the Greek word *disastrato*. Broken down, *dis-* is defined as "torn away from or apart from" and *-astrato* means "the stars." Therefore, a person who is *disastrato* has been separated from the heavenly bodies, or torn from the stars (MacLaine 1983, p. 365).

To know differences and separateness is an important part of consciousness, but now we must also balance this with the feminine consciousness of connection. These thoughts relate to Jung's concept of the unitary reality of the *unus mundus*, or the one world in which all things are connected in the flow of life, where there is a oneness without the blurring of differences. Conscious awareness of the harmony of all life is an expression of feminine consciousness, implying connections, relationships, and similarities. This feminine element is very different from matriarchal consciousness in which all things are fused so that differences and otherness are not seen. The basic symbol of the dog as guide, either as helpful animal leading to the wisdom of the deeper instincts, or as guide to the underworld of death for rebirth, carries with it the idea of connection to something "other." The dog is so like us and yet is other than us. This otherness relativizes the ego and makes us aware of something more than ourselves. This need, which is part of the religious instinct, is the archetypal core of the human-dog bond, and the image of the goddess and her dog is a relevant image for men and women who are working toward greater consciousness and wholeness. You can see inherent in my description of the feminine, Winnicott's idea of *being*, as discussed initially in the preface. The state of *being* contains within it the quality of receiving and incarnating, which is what Ann Ulanov referred to as the transformational feminine.

Robert Bly stated in a workshop given at the New York

Open Center in April 1986 that the way of integration and growth of the psyche is through repetition of the oldest myths and images. I am suggesting in this book that the oldest myths of the Great Mother and her dog are again relevant as a way of integrating that state of being, which implies a connection to the instincts. But it is no longer the ancient She-Wolf, Lupa, the undifferentiated matriarchal feminine with the full power of the archetypal world and the wolf as her companion. But rather, as the result of the necessary and hard-earned consciousness that has taken place, the image of goddess is that aspect of the feminine that can consciously embrace ambiguities and bridge differences by finding connections and similarities in the differences, and her companion is the dog who now carries with it the power of the archetypal wolf but in a humanized way, as friend to humans. It must be remembered that the dog is a friend but is always an "other" and thus carries with it the uncanny, the unknown of the unconscious, as identified by my analysand in dream 3. In this sense the goddess and dog reflect the feminine that carries a connection to the uncanny, the unknown from which something new can develop. It is the image of the part of feminine consciousness, that ability to be completely in the moment in close association with the guide, that brings connection to the instinctual level of otherness within, which ultimately connects us to nature and the otherness outside of ourselves. It is this attitude that will bring us to the awareness of the *unus mundus*.

This book has come directly from my own experience of working with a dog in my office and from what I have learned from this experience. I feel that this material will be helpful to those of us who continue to try to understand the meaning of the feminine and integrate that aspect of ourselves, as well as to anyone who wishes to understand the image of the dog as it comes to us through our own lives or, as here, through the lives of my analysands in the continued process of individuation. I also hope that people like myself who simply love dogs will have a deeper understanding of that bond. Each time we stroke our dogs and in their affection they lick us, we can remember we are participating in one of the oldest healing rituals known to mankind. And we are part of generations of people connected to all that is symbolized by the "goddess and her dog."

Note

1. I am indebted to Mitra Delio for translating this material for me from the original Persian.

Epilogue

Thou passest on the path, if haply thou dost
mark this monument
Laugh not, I pray thee,
Though it is a dog's grave: tears fell for me,
and the dust was heaped about me by a master's hand, who likewise engraved these
words upon my tomb.

Early Greek Epitaph

The preceding chapters have given a brief history of the domestication of the dog, its early connection to religious ritual in the central human mystery of life and death, and the mythologies of Egypt and Greece which expressed this theme. Surely it is not by accident that the dog has become the most popular pet in the world, with over 50 million currently in the United States. With a dog's life cycle being shorter than ours, we have an opportunity to experience through our pet the rhythm of existence, the wholeness and normality of birth, the interdependence of mother and child, youth and the aging process.

This was my experience with Tinsel. I met her first when she was a 2-month-old healthy, friendly puppy. But because I was looking for a fancier dog, one that might have show dog potential, I ignored my instinctive awareness that she was a dog that would make a good companion. I did not meet her again until she was one year old, and, unfortunately, had by then undergone abuse from her first owner. Her friendly openness was replaced by fear, and it took many months for her to trust another human being. Fortunately for me she did, and she became a family dog, a 4-H obedience dog through whom my son could learn mastery and confidence from her love. When I moved into a private office in a building that would allow her presence, she became my co-therapist.

By her presence Tinsel allowed the people that came to see me a unique experience. Because of her absolute gentleness with children, she allowed several of them to experience a large dog without fear, letting them give rides to their dolls on her back, always greeting them with a wagging tail, and joyfully eating any dog treats brought to her—even though at home she was not a dog who particularly enjoyed such treats. She has let curious small children watch her empty her bowels or bladder, whereas at home she is fastidious and very private about these habits. Tinsel instinctively seemed to know when to stand quietly at the chair of someone who was crying, or when to gently put her muzzle into a lap. Analysands who have been with me over the past years have had to watch her slowly become more and more stiff, some days even too stiff to rise to greet them. Because of the gastrointestinal side-effect of the pain medication I used for her increasing arthritis, my analysands have endured or been able to respond in a natural way to the very bad order at times. It was very hard for me to continue working on this book when Tinsel began to deteriorate physically. But I decided to complete it as I felt that there was real value in our experience together and what she brought to the people who worked with me, and perhaps that this experience might lead to a better understanding of our relationship to dogs.

When Tinsel became too ill to accompany me, my analysands also felt her loss. It was very hard for me to make the decision about euthanasia. When I finally did, it was only after this dream.

Dream 7: I was carrying Tinsel in my arms and we were in a large circle of sand at the center of which was a square box in which was a Gila monster. I began to circumambulate the circle in a clockwise direction, moving closer and closer to the center. As I neared the center, the Gila monster leaped forward and struck. At first I was afraid that it had bitten Tinsel on the hind leg, but as I looked more closely I realized that it had passed through the long fur on her leg and it had bitten my left forearm.

This dream, I felt, clearly indicated an initiation process. The fact that there was a circle of sand indicated to me the desert, which is a dry and barren place where inner reflection can take place (as when Jesus spent forty days and forty nights there). My circumambulation of the circle, moving clockwise to the right, I felt indicated a movement toward consciousness. The movement to the center where there was a poisonous animal (which also by its black and pink stripes represented a containing of the opposites as well as the helix, which is the structure of DNA, or life particle), was part of the process of initiation. That the monster struck through Tinsel and bit me meant, I felt, that it was through my experience with her that I contained within me now something more of an understanding of the opposites of life and death.

Tinsel was put to sleep privately by a friend who is also our family veterinarian. But since I wanted to have her remains cremated so that I could place the ashes in a special place in the Blue Ridge Mountains where Tinsel and I had enjoyed hiking, I had to take her body to another veterinary office. Quite synchronistically, at the very moment I walked into the veterinarian's office of the animal crematorium, a black and silver adult female, mostly German Shepherd, was brought into that lobby by one of the technicians to see if anyone knew of a good home for it. The dog had been brought to the clinic to be put to sleep because the owners were moving away and could not take her with them. She was a young dog about four years old, and out of compassion the technician had promised to try to find a home. Lady does have a home now with me. She is a friendly, healthy, obedient dog, who has been wiling to share my life. Patients who liked Tinsel showed some fear of Lady and anger about her presence. They were soon able to understand the anger as part of their grief and the fear as part of their own concern about being replaced when they finished their work with me. The resentment over her presence has been as important as the appreciation of her presence, and she is now an established part of my therapeutic practice. And so the work continues. Indeed, as an old Buddhist maxim has it, "There are no endings, only beginnings."

Bibliography

Agee, James, and Evans Walker. *Let's Now Praise Famous Men.* New York: Ballantine Books, 1966.

American Psychiatric Association. Annual Meeting, Los Angeles, Calif., 1984.

Arkow, Phil. *Pet Therapy.* Colorado Springs: Humane Society of Pikes Peak Region, 3rd edition. 1984.

Arndt, Walter. *Faust: A Tragedy of Johann Wolfgang von Goethe.* Cyrus Hamlin, ed. New York: Norton and Company, 1976.

Auel, Jean. *Clan of the Cave Bear.* New York: Bantam Books, 1981.

_____. *The Mammoth Hunters.* New York: Crown Publishers, 1985.

Bly, Robert. "A Poetry Reading," at the New York Open Center. April 1986.

Boone, J. Allen. *Kinship with All Life.* New York: Harper and Row, 1954.

Bossare, J. H. S. "The Mental Hygiene of Owning a Dog." *Mental Hygiene* 28 (1944): 408.

Bowlby, John. *Attachment and Loss.* New York: Basic Books Inc., 1969.

Bustard, Leo K. "The Animal–Human Bond." *Journal of the Delta Society* 1.1 (1984): 21.

Campbell, Joseph. *The Masks of God: Primitive Mythology.* New York: Penguin Books, 1969.

Cohen, Barbara, and Louise Taylor. *Dogs and Their Women.* Boston, Mass.: Little, Brown and Company, 1989.

Conniff, Richard. "Bloodhound." *Smithsonian* (1986): 65–69.

Dale-Green, Patricia. *Dog.* Chatham, England: W. & J. Mackey and Company, Ltd., 1966.

Davis, Henry P. *The New Dog Encyclopedia.* New York: Galahad Books, 1970.

Dossey, Larry. *Space, Time and Medicine.* Boulder: Shambhala Books, 1982.

Fiennes, Richard. *The Order of Wolves.* Indianapolis: Bobbs Merrill, 1976.

Fogel, Bruce, ed. *Interrelations Between People and Pets.* Springfield, Ill.: Charles C. Thomas, 1981.

Fox, Matthew. *A Spirituality Named Compassion and the Healing of the Global Village: Humpty Dumpty and Us.* Minneapolis, Minn.: Winston Press, 1979.

Franz, Marie-Louise von. *A Psychological Interpretation of Apuleius.* Irving, Tex.: Spring Publications, 1970.

_____. *Interpretation of Fairy Tales.* Irving, Tex.: Spring Publications, 1978.

Freud, Sigmund. "Moses and Monotheism." Standard Edition of *The Complete Psychological Works of Sigmund Freud.* Vol. XXIII. London: Hogarth Press, 1959.

_____. "Three Essays on the Theory of Sexuality." Standard Edition of *The Complete Psychological Works of Sigmund Freud.* Vol. VII. London: Hogarth Press, 1905.

_____. "Totem and Taboo." Standard Edition of *The Complete Psychological Works of Sigmund Freud.* Vol. XIII. London: Hogarth Press, 1913.

Graves, Robert. *The White Goddess.* New York: Vintage Books, 1958.

Hannah, Barbara. Lectures 3-5 from C. G. Jung Institute. Küsnacht, Switzerland: 1953-54.

Harding, Esther. *Women's Mysteries/Ancient and Modern.* New York: Harper and Row, 1976.

Hays, H. R. *In the Beginning.* New York: Putnam and Sons, 1963.

Heiman, Marcel. "The Role of Animals." *Psychoanalytic Quarterly* 25 (1956): 568-85.

Herzog, Edgar. *Psyche and Death.* New York: Putnam and Sons, 1966.

Hillman, James, and Marie-Louise von Franz. *Lectures on Jung's Typology.* New York: Putnam and Sons, 1971.

Jung, C. G. *The Collected Works of C. G. Jung.* Trans. R. F. C. Hull, Bollingen Series XX. Vol. 7: *Two Essays on Analytical Psychology.* Princeton: Princeton University Press, 1953.

_____. *The Collected Works of C. G. Jung.* Trans. R. F. C. Hull, Bollingen Series XX. Vol. 5: *Symbols of Transformation.* Princeton: Princeton University Press, 1956.

_____. *The Collected Works of C. G. Jung.* Trans. R. F. C. Hull, Bollingen Series XX. Vol. 11: *Psychology and Religion: West and East.* Princeton: Princeton University Press, 1958.

_____. *The Collected Works of C. G. Jung.* Trans. R. F. C. Hull, Bollingen Series XX Vol. 8: *The Structure and Dynamics of The Psyche.* Princeton: Princeton University Press, 1960.

_____. *The Collected Works of C. G. Jung.* Trans. R. F. C. Hull, Bollingen Series XX. Vol. 10: *Civilization in Transition.* Princeton: Princeton University Press, 1964.

_____. *The Collected Works of C. G. Jung.* Trans. R. F. C. Hull, Bollingen Series XX. Vol. 14: *Mysterium Coniunctionis.* Princeton: Princeton University Press, 1963.

_____. *The Collected Works of C. G. Jung.* Trans. R. F. C. Hull, Bollingen Series XX. Vol. 6: *Psychological Types.* Princeton: Princeton University Press, 1971.

_____. *The Collected Works of C. G. Jung.* Trans. R. F. C. Hull, Bollingen Series XX. Vol. 16: *The Practice of Psychotherapy.* Princeton: Princeton University Press, 1954.

_____. *Letters,* edited by Gerhard Adler in collaboration with Aniela Jaffé. Trans. by R. F. C. Hull. Bollingen Series XCV. Vol II: 1951–1961. Princeton: Princeton University Press, 1975.

_____. *Word and Image.* Princeton: Princeton University Press, 1979.

Jung, Emma, and Marie-Louise von Franz. *The Grail Legend.* New York: Putnam and Sons, 1970.

Jung, Emma, and Marie-Louise von Franz. *The Grail Legend.* New York: Putnam and Sons, 1970.

Katcher, Aaron. Lecture. American Psychiatric Association Annual Meeting. Los Angeles, Calif., 1984.

Kerenyi, Carl. *Asklepios: Archetypal Image of the Physician's Existence.* Bollingen Series LXV. Princeton: Princeton University Press, 1959.

Kimble, Gregory, Norman Garmezy, and Edward Zigler. *Principles of General Psychology.* New York: John Wilson and Sons, 1980.

Kirch, James. *Shakespeare's Royal Self.* New York: C. G. Jung Foundation for Analytical Psychology, 1966.

Knipe, Rita. "Pele: Volcano Goddess of Hawaii." *Psychological Perspectives,* 13.2 (Fall 1982): 115.

Lansdale, Steven. *Animals and the Origins of Dance.* London: Thomas and Hudson, 1981.

Leach, Maria. *God Had a Dog.* New Brunswick, N.J.: Rutgers University Press, 1961.

Levinson, Boris. *Pet-Oriented Psychotherapy.* Springfield, Ill.: Charles C. Thomas, 1969.

Lopez, Barry Holstum. *Of Wolves and Men.* New York: Scribner & Sons, 1978.

Lorenz, Konrad. *Man Meets Dog.* New York: Penguin Books, 1953.

Luke, Helen. *Dark Wood to White Rose.* Pecos, N. M.: Dove Publications, 1975.

Lynch, J. J. *The Broken Heart. The Medical Consequences of Loneliness.* New York: Basic Books, 1977.

MacLaine, Shirley. *Out on a Limb.* New York: Bantam Books, 1983.

Mahler, Margaret, Fred Pine, and Anni Bergman. *The Psychological Birth of the Human Infant.* New York: Basic Books, Inc., 1975.

Monks of New Skete. *How To Be Your Dog's Best Friend.* Boston: Little, Brown and Company, 1978.

Neumann, Erich. *The Great Mother.* Bollingen Series XLVII. Princeton: Princeton University Press, 1945.

_____. *The Origins and History of Consciousness.* Bollingen Series XLII. Princeton: Princeton University Press, 1954.

Newman, Kenneth D. *The Tarot.* New York: C. G. Jung Foundation for Analytical Psychology, 1983.

Nichols, Sallie. *Jung and Tarot: An Archetypal Journal.* New York: Samuel Weiser, Inc., 1980.

Nurbakhsh, Javad. *Canine Symbolism in Sufi Literature.* London: Khamiqahi-Nimatullahi Publications, 1987.

O'Flaherty, Wendy. *Hindu Myths.* New York: Penguin Books, 1975.

Papshvily, Helen, and George Papshvily. *Dogs and People.* Philadelphia: Lippincott Company, 1954.

Peterson, Rolf. *Wolf Ecology and Prey Relationships on Isle Royal.* National Park Service, 1977.

Powers, Marla, and William Powers. *Journal of Natural History* 95.2 (1986): 6–16.

_____. "Metaphysical Aspects of an Ogalala Food System." *Food in The Social Order*, Mary Douglas, ed. New York: Russell Sage, 1984.

Rilke, Rainer Maria. *New Poems*. Trans. J. B. Leishiman. London: Hogarth Press, Ltd., 1964.

Rynearson, E. K. "Human and Pets and Attachment." *British Journal of Psychiatry* 133 (1978): 550–55.

Sayers, Dorothy. *The Comedy of Dante Alighieri, the Florentine*. New York: Penguin Books, 1951.

Schwartz, Charlotte. *Friend to Friend: Dogs that Help Mankind*. New York: Howell Book House, 1984.

Schwartz-Salant, Nathan. *Narcissism and Character Transformation*. Toronto: Inner City Books, 1951.

Schweitzer, Albert. *Out of My Life and Thoughts*. New York: Mentor Books, 1953.

Searls, H. F. *The Nonhuman Environment*. New York: International University Press, 1960.

Serpell, James A. "Human-Pet Relationships." International Symposium. Vienna: Austin Academy of Sciences, 1983.

Simons, Frederick J. *Eat Not This Flesh*. Madison: University of Wisconsin Press, 1960.

Stekle, W. *Patterns of Psychosexual Infantilism*. New York: Graves Press, 1959.

Time-Life Books. *The Enchanted World of Ghosts*. Alexandria, Va., 1985.

Ulanov, Ann Belford. *The Feminine in Jungian Psychology and in Christian Theology*. Evanston: Northwestern University Press, 1971.

_____ and Barry Ulanov. *The Witch and the Clown: Two Archetypes of Human Sexuality*. Wilmette, Ill.: Chiron Publications, 1987.

Walker, Barbara. *The Women's Encyclopedia of Myths and Secrets*. New York: Harper and Row, 1983.

Walker, William. "Egyptian Mythology." Unpublished lecture, 1984.

Whitmont, Edward. *Return of the Goddess*. New York: Crossroad Publishing Co., 1982.

Williams, Charles. *Taliesin Through Logres*. Grand Rapids, Mich.: William B. Erdman's, 1974.

Winnicott, D. W. *Playing and Reality*. London: Tavistock Publications, 1971.

Woodman, Marion. "Abandonment in the Creative Woman." *Chiron: A Review of Jungian Analysis* (1985): 23–46.

Illustration Credits

Index

Agee, James, 21
Aid Dogs for the Handicapped
Foundation, 33
Ainu Bear Festival, 11–12
American Psychiatric Association
1984 meeting, 3, 15–17
American Psychological
Association 1961 meeting, 16
American Rescue Dog Association,
34
Archaic inheritance, 3, 18–20
Archetype, 2, 3, 4, 10, 23, 24, 47,
69, 70, 71
Asclepius, 25–26, 27, 52, 53
Auel, Jean, 8, 11

Baynes, C. F., 1
Bowlby, John, 16, 21
Bustard, Leo K., 33

Canine Companions for
Independence, 33
Chief Seattle, 7, 70
Christopher, Saint, 40–42
Countertransference, 48

Dale-Green, Patricia, 4
Davis, Henry P., 66
Deer Search, Inc., 35
Delta Society, 22 n.2
Dog
as agent of healing, 25–25,
52–53
in alchemical texts, 23, 37
archetypal aspects of, 3, 4, 10,
23, 24, 47
with autistic children, 3, 33
as companion to the healing god
and goddess, 25
as companion to Isis, 26

as connection to nature, 21
as connection with the instincts,
10, 20, 23, 24, 51, 60–62, 68,
69
as correlation with good health,
32, 33
attachment to, 51–59
with the deaf, 3, 33
domestication of, theories on,
7–9
in dreams, 48, 51, 54, 58, 59, 60,
72, 76
in early religious ritual, 3, 9, 13
eating of, 14 n.2, 41
with the elderly, 3
feminine principle, in relation
to, 62, 69, 70
with the handicapped, 3, 33–34
Jungian view of human-dog
bond, 65–74
in mythology, 23–46
Egyptian, 26–28, 36–37, 39, 40,
45 nn.2, 3, 54, 70, 75
Greek, 25–26, 36, 37, 40,
42–43, 52, 54, 66, 75
Hawaiian, 38, 39
Hindu, 36, 37
Native American, 32, 37, 41,
54
Norse, 36, 43
as used by police (K-9), 34
as used to predict
earthquakes, 35
as psychopomp, or guide, 4,
24, 40, 44, 69
religious instinct, in relation
to, 10, 23, 51, 68
rescue, for, 34
sacrifice of, 10, 11, 13, 14 n.2,
32, 65
seeing eye, 33
Suchi, 1–2
as symbol of first bond, 19–21